Humanism, Morality, and the Bible and Other Essays

Humanism, Morality, and the Bible and Other Essays

David Bruce Taylor

BOOKS

Winchester, UK
Washington, USA

First published by O-Books, 2010
O Books is an imprint of John Hunt Publishing Ltd., The Bothy, Deershot Lodge, Park Lane, Ropley,
Hants, SO24 0BE, UK
office1@o-books.net
www.o-books.com

Distribution in:	South Africa
	Stephan Phillips (pty) Ltd
UK and Europe	Email: orders@stephanphillips.com
Orca Book Services Ltd	Tel: 27 21 4489839 Telefax: 27 21 4479879
Home trade orders	Text copyright David Taylor 2009
tradeorders@orcabookservices.co.uk	
Tel: 01235 465521 Fax: 01235 465555	ISBN: 978 1 84694 376 8
Export orders	Design: Stuart Davies
exportorders@orcabookservices.co.uk	
Tel: 01235 465516 or 01235 465517	All rights reserved. Except for brief quotations
Fax: 01235 465555	in critical articles or reviews, no part of this
	book may be reproduced in any manner
USA and Canada	without prior written permission from the
NBN	publishers.
custserv@nbnbooks.com	
Tel: 1 800 462 6420 Fax: 1 800 338 4550	The rights of David Taylor as author have been
	asserted in accordance with the Copyright,
Australia and New Zealand	Designs and Patents Act 1988.
Brumby Books	
sales@brumbybooks.com.au	A CIP catalogue record for this book is
Tel: 61 3 9761 5535 Fax: 61 3 9761 7095	available from the British Library.
Far East (offices in Singapore, Thailand,	
Hong Kong, Taiwan)	
Pansing Distribution Pte Ltd	Printed in the UK by CPI Antony Rowe
kemal@pansing.com	Printed in the USA by Offset Paperback Mfrs,
Tel: 65 6319 9939 Fax: 65 6462 5761	Inc

We operate a distinctive and ethical publishing philosophy in all
areas of its business, from its global network of authors to
production and worldwide distribution.

CONTENTS

Humanism, Morality, and the Bible

In my time at Oxford (1959 to 1962) the largest undergraduate society was that of the humanists. I shared a room my first year, and the person I shared it with turned out to be an admirer of the humanists. I asked him what was it the humanists offered as a basis for morality. He replied: *Because we are human beings.* I've been thinking about that ever since. He thought, and all humanists seem to think, that they have managed to ground morality in observed 'reality', without requiring any doctrinal grounding for our actions. But they haven't, and that answer shows they haven't; but even more than that, it shows it can't be done.

What sort of human beings was he talking about when he suggested that being human implied moral behavior? Certainly not the actual human beings we daily encounter. We would like them to behave morally, but it doesn't surprise us when they don't. I won't say we expect them to be immoral, but we are certainly prepared, not merely against the possibility, but even the likelihood, that on many occasions they will be. If our morality is based solely on the implications of being human, we have a license to behave as we please; there is no action we could contemplate, however dreadful, but we could very easily find numberless justifications for it in the actions of other human beings.

So when he said we must behave morally 'because we are human beings', it turns out he was not talking about the human beings of actual observation or experience at all; he was talking about his own ideal of how human beings *ought* to behave. On the one hand there is nothing wrong with that, but on the other he no longer has grounds for assuming that religion is to be criticized on the grounds that it exalts doctrine above experience and distorts experience by doing so. It is perfectly true that religion

1

does this, but it should now be clear that humanism does it too; in fact, it is impossible to arrive at any notion of morality without doing it. His notion of human beings turns out to be a fictional reinterpretation of the whole idea of being human and, without that fictional reinterpretation, being human would have no moral implications at all.

So, from that point of view, humanism is just like any other religion; so let us now explore those features which make it different from a religion. Humanism appears solely concerned with the fictional reinterpretation of humanity, while religions tend to offer a reinterpretation of the world as a whole. This creates a clash on two topics important to religion but dismissed by humanism as having little relevance to ethics: the ideas of creation and of providence. For the humanist, all considerations of creation – if indeed it makes any sense to talk about such a thing in the first place – are solely the concern of the scientists. How scientists fit Stephen Hawkings' Big Bang theory into their overall understanding of the universe is unclear to me, but it seems to me they generally take the view (which I accept) that the world of matter is eternal: what they say about it is much like what Christians say about God – that it had no beginning, will have no end, has no borders, and goes on for ever and ever in all directions both in time and space. It is:

... A sea without a shore,
A sun without a sphere;
[It's] time is now and evermore,
[It's] place is everywhere.

Such an understanding of the universe leaves no room for any notion of a creator; and if we dispense with the notion of a creator, we automatically dispense with any notion of providence.

As I say, although never having had any scientific education, I tend to accept this view as being accurate at the level of literal

2

fact. But what worries me is that – here as with all other literal facts – the facts themselves have no moral implications; and, on the other hand, we cannot live in a world without such moral implications. We know how we arrive at them – by offering a fictional reinterpretation of the world around us; but, just because it is a fiction, we have no way of knowing what kind of fiction it ought to be. And here we should note that humanists themselves do not avoid – probably cannot avoid – offering a fictional reinterpretation of the world as a whole. It goes something like this: here we are alone in an indifferent or hostile world, totally left to our own devices, bereft of any help but in ourselves.

Humanists would very likely acknowledge this as the way they view the world as a whole and our relation to it; what they would probably deny is that there is anything fictional in such a view. But even if they are right about that (and I have my doubts), such a view certainly contains moral implications, and those of a rather unwelcome kind. We are all aware nowadays of the enormous threats to our future that we face. In the last century we were chiefly exercised by the threat that we ourselves pose to our future, in that the invention of nuclear weapons had made it a real possibility that we would one day destroy ourselves. Such a fear hasn't gone away, but nowadays it takes second place to another: that our heedless consumption of the earth's resources, and even our sheer numbers will, if continuing unchecked, result in nature itself eventually destroying us; and for the moment we can see no way of bringing either of these things under control. We pass decrees about consumption, but so far these decrees have had little practical effect, and it is hard to see that they ever will have; as regards our numbers, politicians have not yet got round to acknowledging there is a problem here at all, let alone come up with any suggestions about how to deal with it. Yet of the two problems – consumption and numbers – numbers is by far the most pressing: even should we manage to institute effective controls on consumption (which I cannot see happening so long as we continue making economics the supreme goal of human existence), these controls would have no real effect without our also being able to control our numbers.

Another point on which I suspect humanists are right as far as literal truth is concerned is that our morality, like all other aspects of our human behavior, has a biological and evolutionary rather than a supernatural and divine, origin; and this origin I take to be (this is simply a guess, I can claim no real knowledge or expertise in this field) our primitive herd instinct, which in the distant past programmed us, without any conscious decision on our part, to prize the well-being of the species as a whole above our own individual well-being; and that this instinctive 'morality' has been undermined and largely dissolved by our ever-increasing powers of reasoning – so much so that a very large proportion of humanity now finds such a preference incomprehensible. 'Looking after number one' has become the axiomatic basis of their own behavior. It is not claimed that such behavior is moral; rather that morality itself is a weakness that those capable of looking after themselves feel justified in ignoring:

> For conscience is a word that cowards use,
> Devised at first to keep the strong in awe...

It surely follows therefore that the humanist ambition to make morality entirely coincide with reason is entirely wrong-headed: it is reason that has undermined it. There is no simple solution here. The herd instinct is undoubtedly atavistic: it takes for granted not merely that I should be prepared to sacrifice myself for what I see as the greater good – which is unquestionably moral; it also unfortunately promotes a readiness to sacrifice other people with the same end in view. The emphasis on reason has – no question – been a useful correction here, nor would I wish to suggest that humanists are of evil intent; but their ambition to ground morality wholly in reason is wholly misguided. Morality does still require that we be prepared to sacrifice ourselves to the greater good, and reason can offer us no justification for doing so.

One of the more obvious advantages of religion over humanism is that it can replace the psychological basis for morality that reason has largely destroyed: it can create a cultural – artificial if you like – herd instinct, hence its appeal. If I point out that any ideology, and particularly political ideologies, do the same, it will be clear, as humanists insist it is, that this is a double-edged instrument: it can, and frequently does, instigate as much crime as virtue. But the answer cannot be to try and dispense with religion altogether, firstly because it cannot be done, secondly because it is the only real means you have of instilling notions of virtue in the (very large) non-rational section of humanity. This is a problem that secularist society, and humanism in particular, seems to be unaware of – and often, indeed, seems anxious to insist doesn't exist. But it certainly does. To quote a notorious statistic, during last year (2008) there were thirty-seven knife murders in the London area, something which would have been unimaginable fifty years ago. One does not need to claim indoctrination can cure criminality altogether, but there can be no doubt it helps to keep it down; a few terrible examples made of offenders would also help.

Before I leave the topic altogether I would briefly like to return to what I said earlier about our world view. The humanist, I suspect, wants to insist that his picture of man's place in the universe – alone in a hostile, or at least indifferent, universe, so that we are wholly reliant on each other for the help and improvement that we need – is no more than the literal truth. One could, I suppose, concede it is the literal truth, but not that it is no more than that. Look, for instance, at justice. Does it exist? What a very odd question! The truth is (the literal truth?) that it *can* exist. It doesn't exist of itself; it begins to exist when we

5

believe in it. So also democracy: by believing in it, we bring it to pass. This is very like what the New Testament (and in particular, the epistle to the Hebrews) actually means by faith: *Now faith is the assurance of things hoped for, the conviction of things not seen* (Hebrews xi.1). In a similar (though perhaps less literal way) by believing in providence we create an effective sense of it, from which we actually benefit. Let us apply the same notion to the literal 'truth' about our condition as put forward by humanism: it is by believing in man's loneliness in an indifferent or hostile universe we create the sense of it – from which no one benefits. The victory that overcomes the world, it turns out, really is our faith.

Let us now (at last) turn our attention to the other major theme of this essay – the Bible: very old, in many places imperfectly preserved, in many places (particularly in the Old Testament) of doubtful – in some places of hideous – moral outlook. What possible use can it be as a basis for morality? The traditional claim is that it is the directly inspired Word of God, but I doubt if the claim will long survive any one's attempt to actually read it; and I also deeply suspect that many of those making the claim, though themselves sufficiently familiar with it to know how implausible it is, rely on the likelihood that very few of their hearers have much knowledge of it at all; knowledge of the Bible in the modern world is a rare thing even among supposedly dedicated Christians. Academics have such knowledge, but tend to keep it to themselves.

So what use can we make of it? It is in fact a valuable resource. In the first place it is *examinable*. 'The Bible says this', and 'The Bible says that', can easily be checked against what the Bible actually does say; and it will often be found, either that it says no such thing, or (though it may seem to say that) it turns out on examination to mean something entirely different, or (most useful of all) though it does say that in one place, it says something conflicting with it in another. The Bible has most

6

attraction for those insisting we must have moral certainty, but it well illustrates the fact that no such thing is possible.

When I was a schoolboy, it was taken for granted that the moral tradition of the Western world (though that term was much less in use then than it is now) derived from two primary sources: the first was the Bible, and the second was classical paganism, and quite a lot of time was spent in taking us through both. (In the modern world, alas, both seem hugely neglected.) A combination of the two is much better than either on its own: in the classical tradition there is a huge emphasis on intellectual honesty and rigor, but a comparative unconcern for improving of the lot of the poor; in the biblical tradition there is the opposite emphasis – a huge concern for the poor, but an indifferent showing when it comes to intellectual rigor. The contrast between the two traditions has been very persistent: in the nineteenth century, for instance, when there was a huge emphasis on the virtue of philanthropy among the newly rich, those who were little interested in religion tended to concentrate on providing free educational facilities, such as art galleries and institutes, whereas the religious-minded preferred to concentrate on providing subsistence, such as housing, clothing and food. Education is, of course, a very fine thing; but subsistence is even more a necessary thing.

We find Paul in the New Testament constantly inveighing against those who wanted to insist that before anyone could become a Christian, they must first of all undergo the rite of circumcision and become fully committed Jews; Christianity could only follow after that. Unsurprisingly, Paul found this to be a huge obstacle in his attempts to interest the Gentile world in his preaching: the rite of circumcision, for a start, seemed to most Gentiles to be barbaric. In the same way, those in the modern world who insist that those who want to be Christians must believe the whole Bible to be literally true are creating the same kind of obstacle to the wider acceptance of their message. Such a requirement is an absolute impossibility to anyone at all familiar with the Bible, whether Christian already, wanting to be, or even mildly curious; even those who know nothing about the Bible have heard enough – often from those making the claim – to know that the claim itself has to be nonsense.

But if it isn't true, what's the point of it? I suspect all four categories listed above are in the habit of asking themselves that question, and I doubt if any of them ever hear an answer which satisfies. The first point to make is, not only is it rarely factually true, even more important, it cannot simply be treated as a rule book. Even if you try to treat just the New Testament as a rule book, you are then faced with some awkward requirements, the chief of which is perhaps that one of the worst sins you can commit is to eat black pudding! (See Acts xv.20, xxi.25, where the injunction to abstain from blood means to refrain from eating it, and not – as Christians of a certain sort would like to insist – from shedding it.)

The Bible may be only rarely factually true, but it is nevertheless overwhelmingly about history, but a view of history which an actual historian would immediately dismiss as a distortion. (Look back to the beginning of this essay: if you want to find moral implications in the world around you, you have to take a view of it that those interested only in the facts will find distorted.) The Bible is interested in the moral implications of history; for Biblical writers history has a theme, a purpose, a meaning, a goal towards which it is inevitably heading; to actual historians it has none of these things. The theme that runs right through the Bible – both Old and New Testaments – is not the Incarnation, not the Virgin Birth, not the Resurrection; it is the idea that history is the sphere of God's activity in his overriding purpose of establishing the kingdom of heaven on earth. From God's promise to Abraham that *in you all the families of the earth shall be blessed* (Genesis xii.3b – taking the marginal reading) to the closing vision of the Apocalypse in which the new Jerusalem

8

comes down out of heaven to be established on earth, that is what the Bible is about; and it is a truly wonderful theme, and not confined to any one nation or locality. We are all, not merely potentially members, but potentially messengers, of that kingdom; not so much the priesthood of all believers as the apostleship of all believers.

The fact that one does not seriously expect this kingdom ever actually to arrive (though the writers contributing to the Bible certainly did) does not mean there is no point in believing in it or in journeying towards it. We will never actually get there; on the other hand we are not standing still, and we cannot stand still. Either we are moving towards that goal, or we are receding from it: the point of the goal is that it gives point to the journey. Another great advantage of viewing the Bible in this way is that it no longer needs to be 'believed' in the way tradition always demanded; it works perfectly well – probably better – simply through memory rather than actual belief.

It will seem to many that it is impractical to reassert the Bible (particularly the Old Testament) as the basis of moral instruction for society at large. I objected against Humanism that its message was solely directed at intellectuals, and that it left that much larger portion of humanity that is incapable of rational thinking without a moral compass. But for any kind of understanding of the Bible along the lines I have interpreted it there needs to be a grounding in the humanities in general, and in the ancient world in particular, which such people do not have, and would have no interest in if it were offered to them. I accept this is true for society as a whole, and that the necessary knowledge of the Bible as a whole, and the desirable knowledge of the ancient classics, is a qualification for teaching rather than for those one hopes to benefit; just as the doctor has a much more profound knowledge of medicine than his patients do, though he nevertheless stresses the importance of diet and exercise to all of them, regardless of their level of sophistication.

The ancient divide between pagan literature and the Bible is still with us: Humanism would have no qualms about reviving classics in education, but would baulk at doing anything similar for the Bible. Even that would probably be of considerable benefit to society as a whole. But the classics have this obvious disadvantage compared with the Bible: there is hardly any classical literature that you can put before the very young or the comparatively uneducated; but there is a lot of the Bible that you can – which is precisely what Humanism sees as the danger. The Bible as a whole may be fiendishly complex, but it contains numberless individual items which can appeal to everybody – not necessarily as being true, but as being memorable and instructive. That is how it worked in the past, and could easily work again, and to everybody's benefit.

Science and Religion:
A Secular Sermon

Strange is our situation here on Earth. Each of us comes for a short visit, not knowing why, yet sometimes seeming to divine a purpose. From the standpoint of daily life, however, there is one thing we do know: that man is here for the sake of other men – above all for those upon whose smiles and well-being our own happiness depends.
ALBERT EINSTEIN

I'm not the first to have used that text. You'll find it as the motto at the head of chapter 6 of Professor Dawkins' now notorious book, *The God Delusion*. Now spot the deliberate mistake. '*From the standpoint of daily life ... there is one thing we do know: that man is here for the sake of other men ...*'. In fact we know no such thing; indeed, from the standpoint of knowledge we may even be said to 'know' the opposite. There are not many of us who take that view of daily life, and even fewer who act upon it. It's a fiction. Einstein either made it up himself, or is quoting someone else who made it up. It is not an observation of what daily life is actually like; it is an aspiration for what it ought to be like, for what we would like it to be like, for what we must endeavour to make it like. In other words, it is not any kind of fact, it is a doctrine. It is uttered by a scientist – and a scientist of extraordinary repute – but that doesn't make it scientific; it has exactly the same kind of validity as any other doctrine, even those formulated by men who have no understanding of science at all.

This is not to disparage it, though the realization has the excellent effect of negating the criticism scientists (and particularly Einstein himself) tend to make about religion being 'exploded' or 'pre-scientific'. In the sense that religion is exploded, so is Einstein's own pet doctrine. On the other hand, can we manage without it? Einstein's justification of our moral

11

outlook turns out to be fictional, but it does nevertheless offer a justification; and without such a fiction what sort of justification would be have? None. But then, of course, it is by no means the only justification on offer. All of them are fictions, and it turns out, that of itself cannot be held against them; it turns out that if we want to create a system of morality, it can only be done on the basis of a fictional re-interpretation of the world around us. And that's what religions basically are.

The world has been examined by scientists in order to find out how it works, and there is no question but they have had extraordinary success in the enterprise. But in the process of discovering how it works they have increasingly shown us a world that is entirely directed by impersonal forces; and as for being created, it makes little sense to think of it as ever having been created at all. Matter in some form or other has always existed, and always will. Our own world may have had a beginning and may have an end, but the universe as a whole has neither; and the existence of our world, and its eventual destruction, are merely the consequence of those impersonal – one might even call them random – forces eternally at work throughout a mindless universe; it is they that brought us into being, it is they that will bring us to an end. Such a world, such a universe, has no meaning, no purpose, and above all no moral implications.

Being ignorant of all science myself, I am not in a position to pronounce on the accuracy of such a view. On the whole I tend to accept it, but solely on the basis of my ignorance, not at all on the basis of my knowledge. And I do know that there are scientists, some of them quite eminent, that refuse to accept it; but on the whole they come across to me as wishing it were otherwise, rather than actually knowing that it is. So there it is: the world we live in has no meaning, no purpose and no moral implications; and on the other hand we cannot live in such a world. The world we actually live in has to have those features, regardless of whether they are really there or, on the contrary, we find that we have to invent them; and even Einstein has apparently felt that need, and proposed his own fictional remedy.

On what basis do we invent them? As suggested above, not on the basis of what we observe, but of what we hope for. A doctrine sets out the program of how we think the world might be made a better place. Its basis is not therefore rationality. Once we have accepted the doctrine, once we have pledged our loyalty to it, reason can tell us how to go about making it a reality; but reason can never tell us whether the vision we have accepted is a 'true' one. There is no such thing as a true doctrine, or a false one; only an admirable doctrine – or its opposite, a hideous one. And in practice we do not agree, and never can agree, on precisely which is which. Not only were the doctrines of National Socialism sincerely admired at the time, even by some men of undoubted good will, they still are by some – though the revelations of history make it much harder to see them as men of good will now than it was formerly. But we have no need to be extreme as that. In our own day many cling to a vision of capitalism as the only form of society in which the majority of men can achieve true happiness, while others insist that this can be achieved only by a return to socialist thinking – nor is it appropriate to describe either side as right or wrong; a sincere and honest desire to improve the lot of man, to offer the world an eternal salvation, is perfectly compatible with either point of view, and will be found in the members of both 'churches' equally.

Does this mean, then, that any doctrine will do? That's a hard one – so hard, indeed, that I do not think a convincing answer can be offered. Just look at the varieties of the doctrines on offer. Both points of view described above, for instance, would be equally abhorred by those who maintain *as a matter of principle* that the salvation of the planet earth can only be achieved by the complete annihilation of the human race. They do not argue, it may be said in their defence, that their followers should commit themselves to its destruction; they merely observe that humanity itself is hurtling towards that end and can simply be left to get on with it. Our insistence on our human rights, for instance, prevents all effective means of limiting the growth in our numbers; our determination to evaluate our lives solely in terms of economic growth will ensure that sooner or later we will have exhausted the commodities on which we depend for existence. The planet we live on knows nothing of our human rights and is visibly damaged by our mad pursuit of economic growth; the planet itself will sooner or later destroy us altogether – and it is beginning to look as though it may well be sooner.

Let's not go looking for the right doctrine, therefore; such a thing is never going to be found. And I don't propose to try and adjudicate the merits of the countless varieties of doctrines jostling for our attention. And yet on the other hand it will not do to shrug one's shoulders and vainly try to dismiss them all. Without them, as I say, the world we live in cannot be lived in. Think of that world as being rather like a house as it comes to us straight from the builder; in that condition it is uninhabitable. We need fittings in the kitchen and the bathroom; we need furniture throughout the house; we need curtains, carpets, cushions – only then does it become (in the hideous modern phrase) 'fit for purpose'. The world that science has shown us can be seen as the house as it comes to us from the builder; it is the doctrinal system we embrace that makes it possible for us to live in it. I don't here distinguish between a doctrinal system and a religion; they both have the same function; it is on the basis of that same function, therefore, that they come into the same classification. Religions in particular will resent this: they like to insist that they are true. It is perhaps forgivable, since Einstein also though his doctrinal formulation was true.

But there is one comparison that does need to be made. Are all these doctrinal systems equally adequate? Will Einstein's doctrine serve us just as well as – the scientific world would probably say better than – an actual religion? The evidence seems to point to the answer 'no'. Doctrinal systems work almost the same way as does a computer program. We do not spend much of our lives asking whether this course of action is right or wrong; the doctrinal system we have embraced (or been brought up in without ever having questioned) in all but a very few instances tells us that automatically. The essential feature of any doctrinal system, therefore, is its ability to invade and possess the memory of its adherents so that it can work in this way. Religions do this – indeed, if they didn't or couldn't they would soon die out. Political doctrines do it. Einstein's doctrine, on the other hand, seems specifically tailored for the academic community, where alone it flourishes. It demands of its adherents precisely what successful doctrines make unnecessary: that each and every moral decision must be evaluated in the court of reason to see whether it complies with this 'golden rule'. The vast majority of us have neither the energy nor the inclination to devote ourselves to this endless reasoning; and indeed, it is generally acknowledged that a large section of the human race – perhaps a majority, certainly a very large minority – are incapable of rational thought altogether. Most doctrinal systems cater for them; Einstein's spectacularly doesn't.

It is taken for granted in the modern world that you can have morality without religion. In theory perhaps; but in practice it seems you rarely do.

Creation and Darwin's Evolutionary Theory

So out of the ground the LORD *God formed every beast of the field and every bird of the air, and brought them to man to see what he would call them; and whatever the man called every living creature, that was its name.*

(Genesis ii.19)

Like most people, even those who talk quite a lot about him, I've never actually read a book by Darwin. In my youth it is possible I read one or two books about him – it's so long ago now I can't remember. But everyone, even those who've never read a book about him, everyone talks about him. And if you want to be taken seriously as any kind of scientist in the modern world, it is essential that you agree with him. Animal life is as it is, not because that's the way God created it – so that man could give a name to a series of forever separate and forever unchanging species – but because it has evolved into these forms by a continuous process of natural selection. These species are indeed separate, but not for ever separate; they are unchanging, but not for ever unchanging. Most, if not all, species will eventually become extinct, to be replaced by new species which have evolved as a consequence of successful adaptation, through natural selection, to a new environment.

What is the Christian to make of this? Some insist that if the Bible says a thing, then that thing must be true. If Darwin's speculations (as they insist they are) conflict with the passage above, then the passage above proves –with certainty – that Darwin's ideas are mistaken. Others would prefer to argue that Darwin and the Bible are not incompatible: God did not, at a fixed point in time some six thousand years ago, create the individual species we see in the modern world. Evolution was the means God used in order to create the various species.

Despite the clear intention of the second view to be concil-iatory, scientists will no more accept that than they do the first – which, they argue convincingly, scarcely needs discussion. Are there any remotely plausible reasons for insisting that an account, written getting on for three thousand years ago, in a culture to which any kind of scientific investigation was still unknown, must be preferred to an exhaustive survey of the evidence, and a well-argued and coherent theory to explain it? No sensible person, Christian or otherwise, is prepared to take the so-called creationist view seriously. But science is scarcely less charitable to the second view. Why? Because the theory works perfectly well without any reference to God at all, and if the reference to God is not necessary, then it is not allowed. As William of Ockham insisted of old: *Entia non sunt multiplicanda.* If you don't need the added notion, then you must dispense with it: note, not that you may dispense with it, but that you must.

Darwin's theory, unlike the biblical account, had in his own eyes, and has in the eyes of the modern scientist, no moral impli-cations; and it assumes an entire universe which has no moral implications. In the hands of those who are not scientists, on the other hand, it has had definite moral implications, always of an unsavoury nature. It underlay the racial theories which were prominent in the early part of the last century, culminating in the atrocities of the Nazis. It has been invoked to justify every kind of ruthlessness in business and politics, under the banner of 'the survival of the fittest'. It gets us nowhere for scientists to insist that these are abuses of the theory; they are, but such abuses are abound to occur when the absence of any moral implications in the theory is both admitted and affirmed. Just as nature abhors a vacuum, so our human nature abhors a moral vacuum: we do have to have moral implications in the world we live in, whether that world offers them or not. Science insists that to infer moral implications from the world we live in can only distort our understanding of it. To speak more accurately, it distorts our scientific understanding of it; but man no more lives by science alone than he lives by bread alone.

No matter what science says therefore, we have to have an account of the created world that does have moral implications. *And God saw everything that he had made, and behold it was very good* – Genesis i.31a. Darwin had no interest in whether it was good or not; his scientific approach gave him no guidance on the question, which in any case he wasn't even asking; and had he asked it, he would have forfeited the esteem of all his fellow scientists. But we, on the other hand, are bound to ask it.

It's not a question to which we can ever claim to have found the right answer. Science derides religion above all for its tradition of claiming certainty. Science, which deals rigidly with hard, examinable evidence, is aware that all its conclusions are merely provisional; further evidence may – almost certainly will – lead in the future to different conclusions than the ones we currently hold. The very fact that religion claims to have certain and forever unchanging knowledge of what is good and bad, true and false, right and wrong, is itself the proof that religious claims are bogus – that, and the huge variety of such certainties on offer.

Perhaps those particular claims are, and we should look on the Bible as a search for such knowledge rather than a revelation of it. Treated that way its value is unaltered. Its teaching that life is a gift of God, that man is frail and longs for a redeemer, that we are never alone in facing adversity, they may not be truths is any scientific sense, but they are as validated by our experience today as they always have been. And no theory of evolution can ever rob us of them.

Dawkins' Dream: An Atheistic World

'Imagine... a world with no religion. Imagine no suicide bombers, no 9/11, no 7/7, no Crusades, no witch-hunts, no Gunpowder Plot, no Indian partition, no Israel/Palestinian wars, no Serb/Croat/Muslim massacres, no persecution of Jews as "Christ-killers", no Northern Ireland "troubles", no "honor killings"... no Taliban to blow up ancient statues, no public beheadings of blasphemers, no flogging of female skin for the crime of showing an inch of it.' Professor Dawkins must be astonishingly naïve if he believes all this. We don't in fact have to imagine a world with no religion; both Russia and China provided us with an extended view of such a world in the last century, and it in no way corresponded to Professor Dawkins' hopes. Even the French Revolution, though we're not supposed to say so nowadays, perpetrated quite appalling barbarities with the professed intention of replacing religion with the worship of Reason. (It is due to any deity to have its name capitalized.) It is of no relevance to insist that the barbarities of the previous system were commensurate: first of all, they weren't, but even if they had been, the whole point of the innovation is to usher in a more-or-less perfect world, and this has never been known to be the consequence.

It is not the nature of one's beliefs that does the damage, but the blind zeal with which they are put into practice. It is people who are convinced that, for the first time in history, they have found *the* answer to our problems that lay waste all about them. I remember from my own youth a glib revolutionary dogma that you had to break eggs in order to make an omelet. The breaking of eggs was easy (it always is); it was the making of the omelet that was hard, and in the event no omelet ever seemed forthcoming. Milton had a better understanding of revolutionary outcomes: 'New presbyter is but old priest writ large'.

Nor can one allow the plea that the real doctrine has never been tried. For the whole of the seventy years of Communist Russia there were those who admitted things were going wrong, but only because 'real socialism has never been tried'; and however long the tragedy had lasted, this excuse for it could have been – and would have been – made endlessly.

If, like me, you are old enough to have gone through the whole of your school days without ever having had to do any science, there are aspects of scientific thinking that seem to miss the point. Scientists will naturally insist this is because one's education has been lacking; on the contrary, I believe one can successfully argue that the triumph of science has in some ways warped general intelligence. Professor Dawkins assumes throughout the book that if an assertion can be shown to be not literally true, it has no other kind of validity to fall back on. The existence of God is, for him, a hypothesis which is proved to be untrue because of the total lack of evidence in support of it. I agree with that reasoning. There is a convention in argument that it is impossible to prove a negative, but I don't accept that it is: if there is no evidence in favor of the proposition, then that fact is itself the evidence against it – and conclusive evidence. But the existence of God does not need to be viewed as a hypothesis at all, and there are plenty of 'believers' (I shall question even that notion shortly) who do not in fact treat it as such.

But I would like to start with an easier instance of an assertion which is very obviously not literally true, but cannot on those grounds alone be judged to be invalid. Professor Dawkins revives a charming old custom of prefacing every chapter with a motto. The heading to chapter 6 reads:

Strange is our situation here on Earth. Each of us comes for a short visit, not knowing why, yet sometimes seeming to divine a purpose. From the standpoint of daily life, however, there is one thing we do know: that man is here for the sake of other men – above all for those upon whose smiles and well-being our own happiness depends. – ALBERT EINSTEIN

The semi-religious tone of the utterance (I prefer that to 'pseudo-religious') will be obvious to every reader; but the part I particularly wish to draw attention to is the claim that 'there is one thing we do know: that man is here for the sake of other men…' We don't know that at all, nor can the assertion be convincingly described as 'true'. It's a fine and laudable sentiment, and much good may be expected from its proclamation; but it is certainly not any kind of fact. But the really interesting point is that Einstein seems to think that it is, and Dawkins seems to agree with him.

I'm not criticizing the above simply because it is not a fact; on the contrary I take it for granted that we cannot – simply cannot – arrive at any kind of ethical notion without the aid of idealized fictions of this kind – for that is what it clearly is. If we started out on the basis of what we actually observe mankind to be, what we derive from the literal truth would be nothing like what we normally consider to be ethical. Professor Dawkins, if he wants a morality, has to reinterpret humanity in the same idealized terms as we see Einstein doing above. Religion reinterprets the world around us in a similar fashion. When I see the world around me as a gift, and my life within it also as a gift, I am well aware that I am not perceiving any kind of fact; if I worship the giver of the gift, I do not have to persuade myself (unlike Hebrews xi.6) that there literally is such a giver; I am well aware that literally there is not. But which is preferable for the purpose of ethics: science's assurance that the world, and myself in that world, are both of us the product of blind forces to which no providential benignity can be attributed, or my own personalizing of those forces, which enables me to see them as benign and act benignly as a consequence?

I have since my early twenties been perfectly happy with the notion that all religious imagery is fictional, and all gods are fictional beings. I published a book, some forty years ago, which had that as its starting point. (The public, sadly, was not ready for it, and I'm told that most of even the very first binding was remaindered.) This will immediately be taken, both by religionists and their opponents, as an admission that I am not in fact a believer. I don't mind admitting I think the emphasis in Christianity on belief is a big mistake. What I came to realize in my twenties – and it must have been the case for several years before that – was that I placed no emphasis on belief at all. The basis of my own religion was observance and memory, not belief. Once again, both religionists and their opponents will reply that observance has no meaning without the belief. But in fact what really gives observance meaning is the assimilation and internalization of a complex of religious imagery. And it is perfectly sensible, and even perhaps preferable, that the imagery should be absorbed as a consequence of observance, and not as a preliminary to it. I'm fairly sure that was my own religious history; I'm fairly sure it is the real religious history of very many so-called believers.

The endless laudations of science scattered throughout the book had the same kind of effect on me as I imagine the psalms, canticles and anthems that I sang throughout most of my early life would have on non-churchgoers. (From the ages of ten to forty-three I was almost continuously a singer in various cathedral and chapel choirs. And Professor Dawkins, by the way, is mistaken in thinking there are no longer any clerks at New College; if he goes into the chapel during evensong, the gentlemen standing in the back rows of the choir are precisely these same clerks. I believe there are nowadays twelve of them; the development of four-part harmony, not foreseen in the fourteenth century, has necessitated the increase in numbers.) Those of us deeply involved in religion are slow to understand the profound sense of boredom our enthusiasm begets in those not similarly besotted. Professor Dawkins comes across as just such an evangelist; he cannot complain of the epithet, since he himself tells us, 'If this book works as I intend, religious readers who open it will be atheists when they put it down'. He seems to like his atheism as we are told General Booth liked his religion: like his tea – hot and strong; I prefer my religion like my whisky – with ice and water.

Professor Dawkins is exercised by the very high levels of credulity that he finds in America, and wonders how this can be when (a) science, which is incompatible with it, is in such high esteem, and (b) when Europe has seen a record decline in religiosity in the course of the last half century. The second point, I suspect, has to do with levels of welfare payments. It is noticeable that where these are highest, namely in Scandinavia, and particularly in Sweden, religiosity tends to be at its lowest. The fact that welfare payments in America are both less generous and tend to be accompanied by a loss of dignity may have a lot to do with it. The heartfelt prayer of the masses has always been: 'Give us this day our daily bread.' In Europe for the moment this is directed more towards earthly than to heavenly powers.

But on the first point my deep suspicion is that the widespread credulity and the high esteem of science are in fact causally connected. Professor Dawkins wrings his hands over the loss of intellectual innocence; he quotes numerous founding fathers and endeavors to show that for practical purposes every one of them was an atheist. But every one of them had also had a classical education, and that is almost certainly where the problem lies. Already in the eighteenth century voices of protest were being raised against schools wasting their pupils' time on subjects that were deemed to have no practical value: 'We need hands, not heads,' was the cry. The consequence has been that for more than two hundred years the input of the humanities into education has been inadequate, and that is why it is so easy for unscrupulous evangelists to present the Bible as if it had dropped directly out of heaven, and is therefore not to be questioned in any way. Increasingly since the last war the same cry has been heard in Europe also, and already signs of a similar credulity are beginning to appear. The idea that more and better scientific education is the answer here is moonshine; it is much more likely to make the problem worse. If Professor Dawkins wishes to combat credulity, he must campaign for a revival of the study of ancient literature in education – nowadays I suppose (alas) in translation (see I Samuel iv.22) – the Bible, after all, has always been studied in translation. It is essential that pupils should have some wider acquaintance with ancient literature if they are not to run away with popular, but utterly foolish, notions of what kind of book the Bible is.

Professor Dawkins assures us that there must be a purely Darwinian explanation for the phenomenon of religion, because there must be a purely Darwinian explanation for all aspects of human behavior. He may well be right, but he seems to believe that when he has found it he will have somehow exposed religion as an illusion. That's the bit I can't see. If all aspects of human behavior must have a purely Darwinian explanation, then it follows that the astonishing virtuosity of professional musicians (particularly keyboard and string players), the financial genius of multimillionaires, the intelligence and expertise of some academics (including, of course, that of Professor Dawkins himself) must all of them have a purely Darwinian explanation. If we find it, does it in some way 'explode' these activities? No, of course it doesn't; they still remain spectacular and impressive. So how would it 'explode' religion? I suppose Professor Dawkins would argue that it explodes religion's claim to be in some way revealed or supernatural. Well, yes, he can have that: it does. But why should he assume that all religions everywhere claim to be revealed or supernatural? Pagan mythology, for a start, doesn't seem to.

A whole chapter of the book (chapter 6 – the very one headed by the quotation from Einstein discussed above) is devoted to the theme of good works, and how it is perfectly possible to devote one's self to them without any input from religion. That it is possible is certainly true; that religion has had no significant influence here is, on the other hand, demonstrably false. The Professor notes that compassion for the misfortunes of our fellow men (!) is nowadays taken for granted pretty well by the whole of the educated world; and he also seems to admit that it hasn't always been so, but he offers no discussion of how it came about. The typical view of human misfortune in almost all earlier civilizations was that one should try to avoid thinking about it; you will only make yourself miserable, without making anyone else any happier. Intellectual Greeks and Romans were never quite so heartless as that, but even they did not seem to rate compassion highly as one of the virtues. But: 'Religion that is pure and undefiled before God and the Father is this: to visit orphans and widows in their affliction, and to keep oneself unstained from the world' (James i.27). You will find it hard to match that anywhere outside Christianity, not only in the 1st century, but even for one or two after that. Nearer our own time, there was a huge philanthropic effort throughout the western world in the nineteenth century; little if any of it was not inspired by the specifically Christian beliefs of the philanthropists. The observation, though, does exclude benefactors of the arts and sciences, where irreligion often played the larger part. This merely perpetuates a distinction that was noticeable in the ancient world, and again in Europe during and after the Renaissance: the tradition of classical paganism tends to have high standards of intellectual honesty, but low ones of social concern. The Christian tradition is the opposite of this, with low standards of intellectual honesty, but high standards of social concern. A combination of the two is thus to be preferred to either on its own. (Some Christians will protest that there have been some towering intellects among Christian thinkers. I would agree with the criticism that until very recent times they have failed on a most important point: they seem to have viewed their task as being quite simply to defend Christian claims against

25

criticism; they never seem to have undertaken the essential task of questioning the claims themselves.)

'Religion is regarded by the common people as true, by the wise as false, and by the rulers as useful.' Professor Dawkins quotes this on page 276, where he attributes it to the younger Seneca. I am more used to a version by Gibbon, where he tells us religions were anciently regarded by the people as all equally true, by philosophers as all equally false, and by magistrates as all equally useful. Professor Dawkins assumes Seneca is being insincere; I cannot argue because he gives no reference for the quote, but I do know from extensive reading of Seneca that cynicism is not his usual style, and I also know from my memory of Gibbon that he makes the observation with approval of the general air of tolerance that the convention created. He might have added that no magistrate had ever found philosophy of any use at all – not natural, not analytic, nor even moral. The discussion of Hauser's moral philosophy on pages 222-6 makes clear why this is so. I did moral philosophy myself as a special subject when I was an undergraduate, and it astonishes me that so little has changed in more than forty years, or that there has been so little protest about such inanities. Macaulay somewhere observes that no one was ever diverted from anger by reading Seneca's *De Irâ*, and I agree with him. But Seneca's examples are all of them close to the real life of his day – quite unlike Hauser's runaway trucks, points, and sidings, and fat men on bridges, and so forth. So Seneca is far more likely to improve one's morals than Hauser is, even though still not very likely; but stories like the parable of the sheep and goats in Matthew xxv, or of the good Samaritan in Luke x have the capacity to rivet themselves in the memory at a single hearing, and to influence the hearer's behavior, almost without his being aware of it, for ever after.

Throughout the book, but particularly in the later chapters, Professor Dawkins indulges in tasteless and often unfair ridicule both of the Bible and popular religious belief. Those of us familiar with the writings of the Christian fathers, and particularly of the Ambrose/Augustine generation, will be strongly reminded of their equally tasteless and unfair ridicule of paganism. Christian intolerance (which has to be admitted) owes its origins as much to this kind of writing as to anything to be found in the Bible. Should Professor Dawkins' dream of a world from which religion has been totally banished ever come true, it will certainly be as intolerant as Christianity has traditionally been; indeed, to revert to the opening of this article, we have seen such atheism at work and it was.

I should like to conclude by referring to a parable from Luke's gospel, the one known as that of the rich man and Lazarus, which you will find in Luke xvi.19-31. The traditional interpretation is that the rich man goes to hell because he has misused his wealth, and the earlier material in Luke xvi makes it clear that that is how Luke himself understood it; but to the modern critical eye it looks much more interesting than that. That tradition makes the ending ('If they do not hear Moses and the prophets, neither will they be convinced if someone should rise from the dead') sound lame and inconsequential; but it is easy to see a more convincing interpretation. Whoever wrote the parable – and we shall see it cannot possibly have been Jesus – did in fact think the way the tradition interprets him, but that was not the point he was trying to make. Firstly it is clear he was a Jew, which is why he talks of 'Abraham' where he clearly intends us to understand 'God'; and once we've grasped that, the true meaning of the parable immediately becomes clear. So far from being by Jesus, it seems to be an *anti*-Christian parable told by a Jewish opponent. And his message is a profoundly worthwhile one: if you wish to live a virtuous life, the existing religious tradition (Moses and the prophets) already enables you to do so; if you dismiss this as insufficient, then anything and everything will be insufficient, including the miracle of someone rising from the dead. A sensible man can make sense of any religion; the man who cannot make sense of existing religion, but has to have a new one, is sure to repeat precisely the same evils he condemns in Christianity.

Daily Throughout the Year

My text is a little unusual: I no longer have a copy of the 1662 Prayer Book as such, but I do have a copy of the 1928 revision, which contains it. So my text is the opening words of pages 69 and 81. Page 69 reads: *The Order for Morning Prayer Daily Throughout the Year*; and the top of page 81 reads: *The Order for Evening Prayer Daily Throughout the Year*. It is that phrase 'daily throughout the year' that I wish in particular to think about. When I was a boy, even when I was a young man, the idea of Matins and Evensong sung or read every day was completely taken for granted. As a boy I sang Matins (but only, alas!, twice a week on week days), but daily Evensong five times a week; so at the end of four years I had a very good knowledge of the whole psalter, and a fairly wide knowledge of the whole Bible. Today such a plan has the air of an ancient ruin, and the loss is immeasurable. We read the Bible nowadays in tiny little bits which do not connect with each other, which – without a context – seem mystifying and which come across to the hearer therefore as utterly inconsequential. That was how the Bible sounded in the Middle Ages, and Cranmer's intention was to revive the continuous and systematic reading of Scripture so that its genuine message might be heard again, in place of the often fanciful distortions which were the popular religion of the day. He set out his plan in the lectionary which he put at the beginning of the first two Prayer Books of 1549 and 1552; and his labour has not been entirely lost, because the pair of them are easily available in a single volume to this day. When I was young they were published in the Everyman series, and I remember my late sister presenting me with it for my sixteenth birthday; and today the same volume is again available, now published by the Prayer Book Society.

I'll set out the plan, which is so neat and regular that it can very easily be summarized. The most important part is the recitation of the psalter. Cranmer directed that the whole of it was to be recited systematically every month, and to make this happen he divided it into sixty sections, a morning and an evening section for every day of the month up to thirty days. For the thirty-first day, though, he could think of nothing better than simply repeating the thirtieth. Probably most of you can remember having or using a Prayer Book containing a psalter divided up in this way. The one you have in your hands still contains a complete psalter, though without any directions as to how it is to be read: that's a pity. Subsequent Prayer Books do not contain the psalter at all – and that's a disaster; but more of that in a minute.

Then there was the New Testament; once again the plan is simple and methodical. At every Morning Prayer – daily throughout the year – all four gospels, followed by the Acts of the Apostles, were to be read chapter by chapter, so that these five books would be read over in their entirety three times every year. The rest of the New Testament – excluding the Apocalypse, however – would be read in the same manner at Evening Prayer, and these books also would therefore be read over in their entirety three times every year. Of the Apocalypse, Cranmer merely says: '...*out of which there be only certain Lessons appointed upon diverse proper feastes*'.

The Old Testament was a problem even in those days. There are bits of it which no one can deny are not merely dull, but mind-blowingly so: the genealogies of Genesis x and xxxvi, possibly the building of the tabernacle in Exodus xxv to xl, probably the whole of Leviticus except for a very worthwhile chapter xix – when Jesus summarizes the Law with the words, *You shall love your neighbour as yourself*, he is in fact quoting Leviticus xix.18, the second part of it. The two books of Chronicles, together with Ezra and Nehemiah (which are really a single book, and should be called the third book of Chronicles) all contain an awful lot of genealogies and lists of names; at the same time, note this is the only section of the Old Testament that does, giving the lie to the criticism that the Bible is full of 'begats'. Another problem section is the prophet Ezekiel – not so much that he is dull as that he is weird. (Cranmer, by the way, probably thought of the Apocalypse as weird; and I suspect if you sit down and read it at home, you'll agree with him.) Also, Cranmer's Old Testament, you will be surprised to hear, was larger than ours; in his day they hadn't yet thought of the Apocrypha, so what we call the apocryphal books are included in his lectionary; I haven't time just now to explain how the Apocrypha came about.

Cranmer was anxious to get the whole of the reading plan into a single year. If you read the whole of Cranmer's Old Testament right through chapter by chapter morning and evening, the whole task would take just over sixty-five weeks – almost exactly fifteen months. Cranmer had to try and get it down to fifty-two, while also allowing for special readings for special days; he probably found it convenient that some parts of the Old Testament were much less interesting than others.

So that's the overall plan. What we really want to know now is what is the reason for it, what would be achieved by reviving it or something like it; in particular, why this apparently obsessive attention to the psalter. There is, you'll be pleasantly surprised to hear, a good reason. First note that Cranmer, directing the psalter to be recited right through every month, is in fact letting us off quite lightly. The traditional rule for the monasteries – though much neglected by the time of the Reformation – had been to recite the whole psalter right through every week. And throughout history, up until our own day, the psalter has always had this kind of prominence in the reading of Scripture. Why?

The reason for it is not unconnected with the reading of Scripture as a whole, so let's take a quick look at the justification for that. I presume that some of you will occasionally have stayed in hotels, and will have come across a Gideon Bible in the hotel room. Though the intentions are good, I doubt if much good is ever achieved by them. The idea is that men of business, after a frantic and worrying day, will find rest and consolation in reading passages of Scripture; to this end the front of the book contains a kind of index of what passages will address what kinds of anxiety. The passages are usually well chosen; the trouble is that if you are coming to them for the first time, however desperate your need, it is unlikely they will be an immediate or effective remedy. Psalm xxxii.6 tells you why: *Therefore let everyone who is godly offer prayer to thee; at a time of distress, in the rush of great waters, they shall not reach him.* It's not when you're reading the Bible that it saves; it's when you're remembering it. If you already know the Bible, these passages will deliver in a manner that feels almost miraculous; if you are coming to them now for the first time, it is unlikely they will deliver you at all. It is memory here that is the key.

The traditional plan for reading Scripture which Cranmer was trying to revive was not simply concerned with reading it, but more importantly with remembering it: in the words of the collect, he was trying to ensure that we should *read, mark, learn, and inwardly digest* it. And the reason for the emphasis on the psalter was that in the experience of most of those who do read the Scriptures, it is this section above all that has the richest content of memorable phrases and themes which can deliver in the manner hoped for by things like the Gideon Bible. But the Bible as a whole can do it also; hence the wish that we should familiarize ourselves with almost all of it.

Is it to be expected that such a system can be revived? Not by everyone, of course not; it never has been followed by everyone, even by many of those who have an undoubted and strengthening faith. But it can – and should – be revived by at least the clergy; and anyone with any kind of profound interest in literature as well as religion would benefit from it and find their lives enriched and deepened. But what of the rest (and the rest in this case is a large majority); how does it affect them? They may not want to do it themselves, but a lot of them can still find it interesting (to put it no higher than that) to hear it read and to have it explained to them. But for that to happen we need to change our ideas about what sort of book the Bible is. 'The directly inspired word of God' is the traditional claim. If that's what you've been told, if you then sit down to read it you're in for a shock – particularly in the Old Testament, and even in some notorious passages in the Psalms. If God wrote those, he needs to do quite a bit of explaining. So think of the Bible, not as God's revelation of himself to man, but the other way round: think of it as a record of man's search for God, and then those passages which come across to us as reprehensible at least become excusable. I'm not terribly in favour of leaving them out altogether: as we shall see when we come to the psalms for today, as our situation changes, so do the passages of Scripture that particularly speak to us.

There are two approaches to the Bible currently in favour, neither of which seems to me to be satisfactory. One is the typical Evangelical approach, which insists on its being believed to be a true record of all it contains; once again, the Old Testament is an insurmountable obstacle to this approach, but even in the New Testament the miracle stories of the gospels and Acts are just as insurmountable to many people. If you happen to be Evangelical, you may, I suppose, accuse such people of being wrong, but you have no grounds whatever for suggesting they are wicked. On the contrary, it is your insistence on the unquestionable truth of the miracle stories which may be what makes it impossible for many of today's hearers to connect with the Bible at all. A bit like circumcision in the early church: those brought up as Jews took it for granted that without submitting to this rite there could be no salvation; but to the Gentiles, whom Paul was desperately trying to reach, the mere idea of it was stomach-churning. And if Paul had not managed to establish that for

Christians the rite was not required, Christianity as we know it would never have come into existence; it would still be a minor sect within Judaism, that is assuming it had managed to survive at all.

The other approach that will not do is that of liberalism, particularly as professed by the academic world. To them the Bible has become, not so much the basis of the Christian message, as its archeological remains; and a major problem in our modern preaching is that this is how the Bible is put before students at all our Anglican theological colleges. There is undoubtedly a place for scholarship in Bible study, and it is quite right to consider the needs of the preacher as being, for the purposes of scholarship, an irrelevance; but just as the scholar sets asides the needs of the preacher, so the preacher is equally entitled to set aside those of the scholar. Take a tip from the acting profession and its attitude to Shakespeare, which in a way can be considered the actor's Bible. There are such things as Shakespeare scholars, but the actor is very little interested in what they have to say. In the case of Shakespeare, scholars know this and do not object; they realize, for instance, that what keeps the plays alive is the way the actors present them, not the way that scholars do. The truth about Shakespeare is what happens on the stage, not what happens in the study. The actor is well aware that the material is four hundred years old, and makes no attempt to hide the fact; but he believes that, however old the texts may be, they are capable of delivering a direct message to the modern hearer, and that's what he aims to make them do. The preacher could – and should – be doing the same for the Bible; but to be able to do that he must know them thoroughly, just as the Shakespeare actor knows thoroughly the Shakespeare texts. And Cranmer's approach to the reading of Scripture enables that to happen, and a modern selective and anthologizing approach – alas! – does not.

Today is 16th March, and the service is that of Evening Prayer. I will be treating you – I use the word advisedly – to the psalms and lessons as they were appointed by Cranmer for this service. The psalms – hold on to your seats – will be 82, 83, 84 and 85. There are some psalms, as I observed earlier, that are less good than others, and one of them is Psalm 83; but it will also illustrate the point that texts which seem pointless to a particular congregation can seem 'salvational' (to coin a dubious term) to another. Psalm 83 is a prayer offered by a nation terrified of the prospect of invasion from outside. 'Gebal and Ammon and Amalek', or 'the Philistines, with them that dwell at Tyre' mean nothing at all to us, and very little in peaceable times even to Israelites themselves; but if you live in modern Israel, with Hamas and Hezbollah in mind rather than the nations actually mentioned, it would then mean a very great deal. Under Cranmer's plan we began reading the book of Joshua yesterday morning, so the first lesson is chapter iv; and we began reading II Thessalonians yesterday evening, so the second lesson is chapter ii. So now let us begin our service of Evening Prayer as it is to be recited daily throughout the year.

This is the text of a sermon delivered as part of a Lenten exercise to the congregation of St David's, Blaenau Ffestiniog, in north Wales. The date was 16th March 2009, and the Prayer Book used was the 1984 revision of the Welsh Prayer Book.

The Authority of Scripture

The phrase has recently acquired enormous prominence. It is frequently insisted on throughout *The Windsor Report*, and no less frequently in the Evangelical response to it, *Repairing the Tear*. Neither document gives any clue as to how it is intended to be understood. In the Report itself this is no doubt intentional; like the claim that the resurrection was a 'spiritual event', or that same-sex relationships cannot claim 'moral equivalence' with traditional marriage, the value of the phrase lies precisely in it imprecision. It is the kind of assertion that, if delivered *vivâ voce*, would be accompanied with a defiant glare from the speaker, daring any of his hearers to ask him what it actually means. That at any rate seems to be Archbishop Eames' intention in his now notorious Report.

The Evangelical implication seems much less in doubt. They too never state what they mean by the claim, but one is confident of correctly divining their intention. Scripture is a rule book; therefore anything prohibited by a clear direction from Scripture is, without argument, prohibited. There can be no exceptions to this simple rule. St Paul (for instance) has unambiguously condemned homosexuality (and the present writer has no hesitation in agreeing that in fact he has), therefore homosexuality is to be condemned and abhorred by all Christian persons without reservation forever. Those raising questions about the scope of this condemnation (Did he mean homosexual practices, or the simple fact of being a homosexual? Or was he indeed a homosexual himself? – see in particular II Corinthians xii.7-10) are simply trying to undermine the certain truth of the Scriptural command, so that all such questions are as prohibited as the thing itself. To adhere with any rigor to such a viewpoint one has to deny that there is such a thing as a homosexual orientation at all, and logic-minded and zealous evangelicals have no hesitation in doing this: they insist that homosexuality is just like all other sin, simply the product of weakness and depravity on the part of the sinner; and they are also quick to warn less rigorous evangelicals, who are prepared to consider the possibility of such a thing as a homosexual orientation, that they are creating a perilous uncertainty. The propensity to homosexuality is no different from the propensity to any other kind of sin; and Scripture constantly reminds us that we all have a propensity to sin.

It is easy to demonstrate that not even the most ardent evangelical can still claim this kind of authority for Scripture with any consistency. Even in the current debate a glaring inconsistency has appeared: many of those insisting that homosexuality must always be condemned because Scripture condemns it nevertheless have begun to waver on the question whether divorce can be accepted. The Scriptural condemnation here is far more impressive than that of homosexuality, in that Paul, on whose sole testimony (for practical purposes) the condemnation of homosexuality relies, was (like Moses) but a servant in God's house (I Corinthians iv.1, Hebrews iii.3), whereas it is the son of the house – Jesus – who in the Gospel text appears to condemn divorce. But there are no doubt many Evangelicals (and will probably be more, once the above is pointed out to them) who, simply for the sake of consistency, will be as adamant in their condemnation of divorce as of homosexuality; one must therefore turn to the historic record to show them how utterly fictional is the certainty they would like to claim for the authority of Scripture.

Throughout the Middle Ages the Jewish community, detested and reviled by Christian Europe, was nevertheless essential to it, the reason being that throughout that time the Church, on the authority of Scripture, insisted that God prohibited lending money at interest by Christians to other Christians. The Jews accepted the same prohibition (on the basis of the same scrip-

tural texts) with regard to fellow Jews, but felt no such prohibition with regard to Christians. In the Middle Ages, therefore,
much financial business could only be conducted with the help of
Jewish loans; hence their necessity to European city life despite
the hostility with which they were regarded. As commercial
enterprise exploded in the sixteenth and seventeenth centuries, it
came to be felt that, regardless of how Scripture might condemn
the practice, it was essential that the prohibition against lending
money at interest be abandoned – and it was; and no Evangelical
voice has been raised against it in nearly four centuries. Indeed,
it was Protestants rather than Catholics who blazed the trail; and
the more zealously Protestant the businessman, the readier he
was to justify his innovation before God and man.

This proved to be only the first of many such debates between
the authority of Scripture and the practical exigencies of daily
life, almost all of which went against the former and in favour of
the latter. Slave-owners in the eighteenth and nineteenth
centuries fiercely insisted – quite correctly – that the New
Testament uttered not a word of condemnation of slavery; on the
contrary, it set out in detail what the proper relationship between
masters and slaves should be – see particularly Ephesians vi.5-9;
and it was Evangelical Christians above all who eagerly insisted
that slavery was no longer compatible with morality. On the
other hand, in the early nineteenth century the science of geology
was very nearly strangled at birth by the insistence of
Evangelicals that it was inconsistent with what 'we know from
Scripture to be the truth'; and later in the century the same
opposition would be made to Darwin's suggestions about the
origin of species. And on these last two points not all Evangelicals
have yet given way; but I feel confident that the authors
concerned in producing *Repairing the Tear* would be embarrassed
to have it pointed out that their insistence on the authority of
Scripture obliged them to accept, for instance, Creationism. But if
they don't, their position certainly lacks rigor.

'The authority of Scripture' has clearly become a largely meaningless phrase. It survives in the language of officialdom only because of a steadfast refusal to consider what it means, and in popular usage because of a determination to obliterate all memory of its numerous defeats throughout history. We need a new slogan to describe the relationship between Scripture and the Church which claims to be based upon it: and I suggest 'the influence of Scripture' would be truer to actual experience. Paul tells us that 'the law was our *pædagôgos* to bring us to Christ' (Galatians iii.24), and I am tempted for the moment to use the AV mistranslation of *pædagôgos* as 'school-master'. For those wedded to the notion of 'the authority of Scripture' we are still under a schoolmaster, and always will be. Those who want to refer to 'the influence of Scripture' would prefer to think of Scripture as being more like a parent. Both schoolmasters and parents insist on being listened to, but in different ways; both have to maintain discipline, but it is not the same kind of discipline. A schoolmaster cannot afford to let his pupils get as close to him as a parent would naturally like his children to be. A schoolmaster has to maintain discipline at all costs; a parent also has to maintain discipline, but certainly not at all costs. A disciplinarian parent is a failed parent; a schoolmaster over-anxious to be loved by his pupils is a failed schoolmaster. A schoolmaster cannot (often) afford to admit to his pupils he is wrong; a reasonable parent can and does do that without loss of authority. A schoolmaster insists on being obeyed; a parent gives advice which he honestly believes to be good, but accepts that his children sometimes will, and sometimes ought to, reject it.

The idea that Scripture is a kind of rule-book, therefore, is not appropriate. It is much more in the nature of a value-system, which will be clearly seen if we contrast it with that other great value-system on which, like the two central pillars in the temple of Dagon, the entire outlook of what we call Westernism is built

– the pagan classics. Christianity has always been divided in its attitude to this other great, and earlier tradition, some maintaining there is a total incompatibility of the Gospel of Christ with the 'profane tales of the pagans':

> What fellowship has Christ with Belial? Or what has a believer in common with an unbeliever? What agreement has the temple of God with idols?
> (II Corinthians vi,15-16a)

It is to the shame of the Ambrose/Augustine 'axis' that they advocated such a point of view, despite the fact that both of them were fully trained in classical literature, and certainly knew better. One gets the impression that they spoke other than they knew, as men 'who had understanding of the times, to know what Israel ought to do'. Either wittingly or unwittingly they helped to strengthen a tendency in the Christian tradition towards all that is narrow, peevish and morose. Fortunately, the contrary view, though rarely the prevailing one, has never been totally overthrown – until modern times, that is, with the virtual disappearance of the classics altogether from education. This is that the outlook encouraged by a knowledge of the classics is of enduring value, and so must be combined with, rather than replaced by, the Christian gospel. The combination of the two (though Christian supporters of the classics were never quite bold enough to put it this way) is better than either on its own. The classical tradition has high standards of intellectual honesty, but a rather low one of social concern; Christianity, on the other hand, has high standards of social concern, but a rather low one of intellectual honesty. By combining the two one hopes to combine high standards of intellectual honesty with high standards of social concern, which is the basic formula for what we call Westernism.

There are three functions that a knowledge of Scripture has

traditionally been held to perform: (a) it provides the reader with knowledge of what he must believe if he is to be 'saved'; (b) it gives him divinely sanctioned directions for leading a virtuous life (which is an essential part of being saved but by no means the whole of it); and (c) it provides nourishment for the 'soul', so that in times of adversity one need never feel utterly overwhelmed. We shall examine each of these in turn, but by far the longest examination will be that of 'salvation'.

The term 'salvation' is yet another that is often in the mouths of Christians but rarely examined for its meaning, and more than occasionally seems to be used without having any discoverable meaning at all. Its origins, on the other hand, seem to be perfectly clear and intelligible – one could almost say tangible. The biblical idea of salvation derives originally from the time of Hezekiah (715 to 686 BC); it was then that the Assyrians, under Sennacherib, invaded and overran Judah and threatened the city of Jerusalem. We cannot tell with certainty from the record whether the city was taken or not; the Assyrian account says it was, the biblical one that it wasn't – except that II Kings xviii.13-16 seems to be in conflict with what we read in the rest of that chapter and the following one. But in either case it is easy to see the meaning of:

> And the surviving remnant of the house of Judah shall again take root downward, and bear fruit upward; for out of Jerusalem shall go forth a remnant, and out of Mount Zion a band of survivors. The zeal of the LORD will do this.
> (II Kings xix.30-31)

especially when we compare it with:

> In that day the remnant of Israel and the survivors of the house of Jacob will no more lean upon him that smote them, but will lean upon the LORD, the Holy One of Israel. A

remnant will return, the remnant of Jacob, to the mighty God.
For though your people Israel be as the sand of the sea, only a
remnant of them will return.

(Isaiah x.20-22a)

or:

We have a strong city; he sets up salvation as walls and
bulwarks.

Open the gates, that the righteous nation which keeps faith
may enter in.

(Isaiah xxvi.1b-2)

This last may look enigmatic to the inexperienced reader, but is
in fact clear: the Assyrians have overrun the country; those who
want to be 'saved' must be ready to abandon farm, village and
possessions, and take refuge on Mount Zion, that is, the city of
Jerusalem. Any that are not prepared to make that sacrifice and
leave all behind them will be destroyed by the Assyrians. Once
the crisis is over, the remnant that have survived on Mount Zion
will go forth and repossess the land. That gives us a clear and
utterly intelligible meaning for the idea of salvation, and the
imagery which it has generated survives in Christian discourse to
this day. One need only look at the well-known hymn 'Glorious
things of thee are spoken,' and in particular at the concluding
couplet of the first verse:

With savation's wall surrounded,
Thou may'st smile at all thy foes.

or the second verse, which very cleverly exploits one of the
measures Hezekiah appears to have taken to anticipate the siege
of Jerusalem, by diverting waters from the river Gihon to bring
water into the city (II Kings xx.20), and turns it into an image of

abundant grace:

> See, the streams of living waters,
> Springing from eternal love,
> Well supply thy sons and daughters,
> And all fear of want remove:
> Who can faint while such a river
> Ever flows their thirst to assuage?
> Grace which, like the Lord the Giver,
> Never fails from age to age.

One of the conspicuous failings of the whole Christian tradition is that one is never allowed to evaluate any part of it simply as imagery; it has to be affirmed as some kind of certain truth. The above is transparent and appealing as imagery, but how can it seriously be regarded as true?

In the New Testament salvation is again regarded as salvation from the imminent threat of destruction. The first sermon that Peter delivers in Acts is given in ii.14-36, and concludes thus:

> This Jesus God has raised up, and of that we all are witnesses. Being therefore exalted at the right hand of God, and having received from the Father the promise of the Holy Spirit, he has poured out this which you see and hear [*namely, the gift of 'speaking with tongues' which has just been manifest in the disciples*]. For David did not ascend into the heavens; but he himself says,

> 'The Lord said to my Lord, Sit at my right hand,
> till I make thy enemies a stool for thy feet.'

> Let all the house of Israel therefore know assuredly that God has made him both Lord and Christ, this Jesus whom you crucified.

The quotation is from Psalm cx, which is here held to be a prophecy of Jesus' imminent return to earth to set up his kingdom. There is little doubt that the expectation of this event which we find throughout the New Testament (where it is in fact the most important doctrine of all – more important than the resurrection, though you would never guess it from the later Christian tradition) authentically derives from Jesus' own teaching, particularly as we find it in Mark ix.1:

> And he said to them, 'Truly, I say to you, there are some standing here who will not taste death before they see the kingdom of God come with power.'

Paul, for instance, throughout I Corinthians vii, is clearly expecting Jesus' return quite literally 'any time now':

> I mean, brethren, the appointed time has grown very short; from now on let those who have wives live as though they had none, and those who mourn as though they were not mourning [*because the people they are mourning will shortly be raised again to life when Jesus returns to earth*], and those who rejoice as though they were not rejoicing [*because whatever it is they are rejoicing about will no longer have any significance after Christ's appearing*], and those who buy as though they had no goods, and those who deal with the world as though they had no dealings with it. For the form of this world is passing away.
> (I Corinthians vii.29-31)

It is this imminent event which is being announced in Peter's sermon above, and (so Peter tells the crowd) they will find a description of what this visitation is to be like above all in Psalm cx. His hearers, unlike his modern readers, all knew the psalm pretty well off by heart, and in particular:

He will execute judgment among the nations, filling them with corpses; he will shatter chiefs over the wide earth.
(Psalm cx.6)

It is this knowledge of the psalm that strikes terror into Peter's hearers:

Now when they heard this they were cut to the heart, and said to Peter and to the rest of the apostles, 'Brethren, what shall we do?'
(Acts ii.37)

They are asking to be saved from the destruction that Jesus will be visiting on all who do not belong to his kingdom when he finally returns to set it up.

The trouble here, of course, is that the threatened return never actually materialized. In Isaiah's time a lucky few did actually experience the salvation of which he speaks; but two thousand years later we are still waiting for the salvation that Paul took absolutely for granted was imminent. We have good reason to think that his expectation of when Jesus' return would be changed in the course of his life-time. At one time he seems to have assumed that *all* baptized and believing Christians were destined to be still alive at Jesus' coming:

Whoever, therefore, eats the bread or drinks the cup of the Lord in an unworthy manner will be guilty of profaning the body and blood of the Lord... *That is why many of you are weak and ill, and some have died.*
(I Corinthians xi.27, 30)

But in the very famous description of the resurrection of the dead that we find in I Corinthians xv.35-58, Paul no longer seems to see any difficulty in the fact that some faithful Christians have died before Jesus' return; in fact he seems to have hit on this notion of the resurrection of the dead precisely as a solution to that particular problem. But we should also note that even in I Corinthians xv he never doubts that he, and many of his hearers, will still be alive when Jesus returns:

> We shall not all sleep, but we shall all be changed, in a moment, in the twinkling of an eye, at the last trumpet. For the trumpet will sound, and the dead will be raised imperishable, and we [*who are still alive*] shall be changed.
> (I Corinthians xv.51b-52)

or again:

> For this we declare to you by the word of the Lord, that we who are alive, who are left until the coming of the Lord, shall not precede those who have fallen asleep.
> (I Thessalonians iv.15)

(There are two critical points to note here. The first is that if Paul originally believed, as he seems to have, that all baptized followers of Jesus were going to survive until his return, and that any that did not survive were being excluded from the kingdom because of their unfaithfulness, it is possible that this was in fact Jesus' original prophecy. Even Mark's gospel, our earliest, seems to have been written about thirty years after Jesus' death. Many conspicuously faithful Christians will have died in the interval, and it is likely that the prophecy that Mark records has in fact been modified to get round this difficulty. The second is: I have assumed that I Corinthians xi dates from early in Paul's ministry, and that I Corinthians xv is very much later. Although the New Testament contains only two letters by Paul to the Corinthians, when we actually read them it is clear that both of them are collections of fragments of letters that were originally many more than two; and these fragments, of course, are likely to be of varying date.)

The problem for the whole notion of salvation created by Jesus' failure to return was beginning to be felt even in New Testament times. The latest document is already aware of it, and tries to solve it with an obvious equivocation:

> First of all you must understand this, that scoffers will come in the last days with scoffing, following their own passions and saying, 'Where is the promise of his coming? For ever since the fathers [*i.e. the first generation of Christians who had actually known Jesus*] fell asleep, all things have continued as they were from the beginning of creation.'... But do not ignore this one fact, beloved, that with the Lord one day is as a thousand years, and a thousand years as one day. The Lord is not slow about his promises as some count slowness, but is forbearing toward you, not wishing that any should perish, but that all should reach repentance.
>
> (II Peter iii.3-4, 8-9)

There are Christians to this day who insist that this is the answer, and who claim to believe in all seriousness that Jesus will one day return to earth. Some may be sincere – therefore perhaps not entirely sane; but it is likely that many of them are not sincere.

The Church as a whole has looked for another solution to this problem of salvation in the notion of there being a life after death. It will surprise some readers to be told that such a notion is not, on the whole, a New Testament idea at all. The Apocalypse has an emergent idea of it, but even in the Apocalypse it is only after Jesus' return to earth that rewards and punishments begin; and the New Jerusalem, in which those rewarded will enjoy the life of bliss, has a heavenly origin, it is true, but then comes down out of heaven to be set up on earth. Pretty well the only clear delineation of a life after death in the New Testament is the parable of the rich man and Lazarus in Luke xvi.19-31, and that can very easily be shown to be not a parable of Jesus at all, but an anti-Christian Jewish fable. The real point it is making is that if you want to live a virtuous life, the existing religious tradition (i.e. Moses and the Prophets) gives you all the help you need to do so; and if that is not enough, then nothing will be enough, not even someone's resurrection from the dead.

We have seen above that Paul has little space in his thinking for any kind of life after death of the kind that Christianity has traditionally talked about. In his belief the dead are as dead as death can make them until they are once again raised out of death by Jesus at his return to earth. Jesus' own thinking is harder to fathom. If we are right in believing that Paul originally thought that all faithful Christians would still be alive at Jesus' return to earth, and that this idea probably reflects Jesus' own prophecy, then Jesus also has no beliefs about a life after death since – absolutely literally and not at all in the mythological or metaphorical sense that Christianity has subsequently taught – Jesus' own death has abolished death. And it is quite likely that this was at any rate a *part* of his thinking; but difficulties arise when we look at passages like Mark xii.24-27:

> Jesus said to them, 'Is not this why you are wrong, that you know neither the scriptures nor the power of God? For when they rise from the dead, they neither marry nor are given in marriage, but are like angels in heaven. And as for the dead being raised, have you not read in the book of Moses, in the passage about the bush, how God said to him, 'I am the God of Abraham, and the God of Isaac, and the God of Jacob'? He is not God of the dead, but of the living; you are quire wrong.

(Let us first make the point that we are here asking about what Jesus himself believed, rather than about what actually is the case.) If Abraham, Isaac and Jacob are now alive (and in heaven?), when were they raised? And is their resurrection to be conceived as having happened immediately upon their death? *In this passage*, therefore, it is hard to avoid a conclusion which would give us a view of resurrection not unlike the traditional doctrine of life after death.

But even such a view of salvation, the reception of the faithful Christian into heaven after death, has problems for large numbers of contemporary Christians who, if they are honest with themselves, no longer believe in any life after death at all. Some are even finding the courage to say so, and it should be made clear to all the rest that there is nothing immoral or reprehensible in such an admission. Far more blameworthy is the attempt of traditional enthusiasts to intimidate their fellow Christians, to force them to say things other than they actually believe: 'If you don't believe in a life after death, then you're not a Christian at all'. The real meaning of such an 'argument' is: 'We know the belief is doubtful; that's exactly why we are going to insist upon it.'

What meaning can the word 'salvation' have for Christians who think thus? It is, of course, possible that it has no meaning at all for them, and if that is so, no useful purpose is served by insisting on the term. But I think we can arrive at a still valid meaning, which I hope to demonstrate in the conclusion of this discussion. In the meantime we are left with our three original questions: (a) what sort of knowledge do we find in Scripture?; (b) what kind of direction for a virtuous life?; and (c) what kind of support and sustenance in times of adversity or stress?

The tradition seems to imply that the knowledge that Scripture imparts is easily its most important function; in fact it seems to be the least important. Let us look at the Old Testament first, where the overall intention is very much clearer. The central event is the destruction of Jerusalem in 586 BC. At the time – and at all times for the hard-nosed historian – this event was the utter disproof of everything that Israel had ever believed about itself. It was supposed to be a nation chosen by God to fulfill his purpose of transforming the world he had created from what seemed to be its permanent state of corruption into a world of righteousness and justice; such a world the Bible calls 'the kingdom of God', and it was understood to be Israel's destiny to be God's chosen instrument in setting up this kingdom. This destiny was made clear from the very start in God's instruction to Abram:

'Go from your country and your kindred and your father's house to the land that I will show you. And I will make of you a great nation, and I will bless you, and make your name great, so that you will be a blessing. I will bless those who bless you, and him who curses you I will curse; and in you all the families of the shall be blessed [*taking the reading of the RSV margin*].
(Genesis xii.1b-3)

II Samuel vii comes across to the modern reader, not so much as an oracle from the mouth of God, more like a piece of royal propaganda, in which the Davidic house now puts forward its own claim to be God's instrument in transforming history from rebellion against God into conformity to his will. And we can tell, in particular from the prophecies both of Isaiah (xvi.4b-5, xxxvii.33-35, lv.3-5) and of Jeremiah (xvii.24-26, xxiii.5-6, xxx.8-9, xxxiii. 14-22) that Israel bought heavily into the whole of this ideology – a divinely appointed royal house, a divinely created royal temple, a divinely protected royal city; and the whole illusion came crashing down with the fall of Jerusalem to the Babylonians in 586 BC.

The original impulse behind the creation of what we now know as the Old Testament seems to be the determination to maintain that what happened in 586 BC, so far from being the disproof of Israel's divine mission, was in fact a necessary stage in its fulfillment. Looked at calmly and dispassionately the idea seems wildly unreal, and it is; but what the Old Testament is trying to do for the people of Israel is the same as what all religions are trying to do for their adherents. We live in a world which has no meaning and no purpose; but we are creatures of meaning and purpose, and therefore cannot live in such a world; and what religion is trying to do is to reinterpret the world so that it now appears to have that meaning and purpose which in reality it lacks. If religions were true – any religion – they simply could not help us.

The idea is not a new one. The sophisticated part of the modern world will read the above, nod its head wisely and say, 'I told you so'; and the unsophisticated part will for that reason insist that it can't be true, that to admit that religion is unreal is to accept the inevitability of irreligion. But to me at any rate, so far from being a disproof of religion, that is in fact its vindication. We may well believe scientists when they tell us that we live in an utterly meaningless, utterly uncaring universe, but we certainly cannot live by the notion; religion gives us the contrary ideas that we can live by. It cannot make any truth claims, indeed it can justly be accused of distorting the truth, but it nevertheless provides an indispensable service. The Old Testament seizes on history as the field of God's activity, the process by which he will eventually inaugurate his kingdom on earth; and yet it is perfectly evident to anyone reading the Old Testament that the historical narrative throughout is wildly distorted.

When I was an undergraduate there was a prevailing notion that the 'true' meaning of the Old Testament could be uncovered by detecting the distortions and correcting them. Nothing could be further from reality. It is the distortions that are the point of it; if we get rid of them (and it can very largely be done) we are left with a narrative, true to history certainly, but totally without power to redeem the hearer. And the New Testament does the same for Jesus' life and death as the Old Testament does for the fall of Jerusalem. The resurrection is not a true notion – to many readers that will be obvious; but it makes possible the worship of his memory, it gives point to our intense interest in his life and teachings, and above all it offers us a path to *redemption*, to the feeling that however downcast we may sometimes feel, we need never feel that we are utterly abandoned. But this is a feeling, and not knowledge; the only knowledge we need to derive from reading the Bible is the knowledge that in a sense we really are being 'had'.

We are left with two themes, both of which are of the highest importance to Christian life. Neither of them derive so much from the authority of scripture as of its inherent power to persuade. The first is the directions it gives for a virtuous life and the power of its exhortation to embrace it; the second the supplying of that inner strength which comes to one's rescue when the world around you seems to have abandoned you. On the first point the New Testament will to most of us seem much more relevant than the Old: the God of the Old Testament comes across to the modern reader as being far too vengeful and irascible to be a useful inspiration in the practice of Christian virtues. (For a short period I was a schoolteacher in Scripture. I vividly remember one of my pupils, when considering the story of Exodus xxxii and God's anger at the worship of the golden calf, remarking, 'Just like him – anyone else would have laughed!') Surprisingly, though, when it comes to the second point the Old Testament is much richer in the relevant material than the New.

Even the use of the New Testament can be abused, and too often has been. There has always been a certain kind of Christian for whom God's condemnation has brought joy, his forgiveness nothing but disappointment. If you want to know Jesus' own attitude to that kind of religion, you cannot do better than learn up Matthew xxiii. When Jesus said (Matthew xi.28), 'Come to me, all who labor and are heavy laden, and I will give you rest... For my yoke is easy, and my burden light' – assuming he did say it, then he almost certainly meant it literally; he did *not* mean, 'At first sight my yoke is hard and my burden heavy, but once you've accepted what appear to the unredeemed to be harsh rules and heavy duties, *then* you will find true rest'. This is merely an example of something else that Jesus condemned, but that many of his followers love:

'You have a fine way of rejecting the commandment of God, in order to keep your tradition.'
(Mark vii.9)

Those who go through the New Testament picking out Matthew xxvii.25 with which to belabour Jews, or Romans i.24-27 with which to belabour homosexuals, or I Corinthians xiv.35b-36 with which to belabour women, or Ephesians vi.5-9 to justify an institution like slavery – and one could go on a lot longer – are not preaching Christ's religion or anything like it. Let them rather meditate on Matthew v-vii (the Sermon on the Mount), or Galatians v 16-26, or Philippians iv.8-9, and thus learn virtue. Critics will point out that the very existence of the passages I have listed above are proof that even the New Testament is an imperfect book, and I agree that it is. If you want a perfect book, you will have to write it yourself, and I doubt if the result will be anything like as good as the New Testament.

The suggestion that the Old Testament is much richer than the New in the kind of material that keeps one afloat in troubled times will be a surprise to many readers, the main reason for that being that not many even of the clergy nowadays bother to read it. Yet the Old Testament was all that Jesus had to sustain him in the garden of Gethsemane. And it was the Old Testament that Paul in his missionary journeys was bringing to the Levant and making Christians on the basis of it; he had yet to get round to writing the New. Still to this day it offers rich material as the basis of prayer, superlatively of course in the Psalms (which also the clergy seem to have given up reading – no wonder they make such a poor showing in the modern world). It is no accident that from earliest times until the very recent past Christian institutions placed a heavy emphasis on the regular reading of the Psalter in course. The aim was – or perhaps I should say the result, because the intention may have been rather different: the idea of an offering to God rather than the strengthening of one's own soul – the result was a memory filled with a store of little tags constantly spilling out from the unconscious into the conscious mind and providing an unceasing encouragement to engage with the world and overcome it.

With this I complete my outline of the way Scripture ought to function in the Church. It has little connection with the implications of the phrase with which we started, 'The Authority of Scripture', but nevertheless allots a far from negligible role to Scripture, both in directing the Church and strengthening its members. For it to function in this way, it would be necessary for the apparently discontinued practice of daily, methodical reading of Scripture be revived; indeed, the one point on which I do happen to agree with the conservative critics of liberal Anglicanism is the apparent ignorance and neglect liberals seem to exhibit of Scripture. But I hope I have also shown that a revival in the knowledge of Scripture by no means implies the kind of inflexible attitudes which they insist are the necessary, or the only possible, outcome.

Religion and Reality

Consider the following passage from Exodus:

> Then Moses stretched out his hand over the sea; and the LORD drove the sea back by a strong east wind all night, and made the sea dry land, and the waters were divided. And the people of Israel went into the midst of the sea on dry ground, the waters being a wall to them on their right hand and on their left. The Egyptians pursued, and went in after them into the midst of the sea, all Pharaoh's horses, his chariots, and his horsemen. And in the morning watch the LORD in the pillar of fire and cloud looked down upon the host of the Egyptians, and discomfited the host of the Egyptians, clogging their chariot wheels so that they drove heavily; and the Egyptians said, 'Let us flee from before Israel; for the LORD fights for them against the Egyptians.'(Exodus xiv.21-25)

A miracle? If you examine the passage carefully, we can't be totally sure. 'The LORD', we are told, 'drove the sea back by a strong east wind all night, and made the sea dry land, and the waters were divided.' There doesn't seem to be any miracle there unless, like Cecil B de Mille, we are determined to see one. But when the account goes on to tell us that the waters were a wall to the Israelites on their right hand and on their left, we can see that Mr de Mille was by no means the first to view the event with an over-heated imagination. Also the idea of two walls of water collapsing onto the Egyptians does not seem to be the earliest version of the story. If we assume that unusual weather conditions created a fordable passage in the sea, which seems to be the earliest version of the story, then the account of the Egyptian disaster becomes equally plausible. Although they were in chariots and the fleeing Israelites on foot, the sea bed was essentially soft ground – which little hindered the Israelites as they fled, but made it all but impossible for the much heavier Egyptian chariots to proceed; with the result that when the weather changed and the sea returned to its normal state, the Egyptians were unable either to go forward or back. Hence the calamity.

Probably most of us here, at some stage in our school days, were told in connection with one of the biblical miracles – perhaps with all of them! – that what 'really' happened was something quite unmiraculous in itself; and some of us may even have been reminded of Shaw's (to me utterly unconvincing) dictum that a miracle is an event which creates faith; against which one must insist that that is not what the word miracle has ever meant in the past, nor does it carry any conviction in the present. All of us, believers and unbelievers alike, recognize a miracle story from our perception that the alleged event can never really have happened – which, to the traditional believer is proof it was God that did it, to the rest of us that a perfervid imagination has been at work. Our teachers no doubt meant well – were probably in fact quite right; but they were still missing the real point.

The same point could be illustrated with another detail of the Exodus: the pillar of cloud by day and the pillar of fire by night. Here its first mention:

> And the LORD went before them by day in a pillar of cloud to lead them along the way, and by night in a pillar of fire to give them light, that they might travel by day and by night; the pillar of cloud by day and the pillar of fire by night did not depart from before the people.
> (Exodus xiii.21-22)

If we had only this account, no one could have any difficulty with it. The Israelites set out towards an erupting volcano, which they can see in the distance as a column of smoke during the day and a column of fire during the night. Where's the miracle in that?

56

Quite!, said the priestly authors to themselves, and were determined to remedy the deficiency:

> Then the angel of God who went before the host of Israel
> moved and went behind them; and the pillar of cloud moved
> from before them and stood behind them, coming between
> the host of Egypt and the host of Israel. And there was the
> cloud and the darkness; and the night passed without one
> coming near the other all night.
> (Exodus xiv.19-20)

That's better – now we have a real miracle.

At the risk of overdoing it, I would like to add just one more example, which relates to Moses striking the rock to give water to the Israelites. The incident is related twice in the Exodus story: the first time at the very beginning of the journey in the wilderness, in Exodus xvii.1-7, and the second time at the very end of it in Numbers xx.2-13. It is undoubtedly this repetition of the incident which accounts for Paul's extraordinary claim in I Corinthians x.4 that 'they drank from the supernatural Rock which followed them, and the Rock was Christ'; that is to say, it was one and the same miraculous Rock that Moses struck first of all in Exodus xvii, and again in Numbers xx, and he could do this because the Rock miraculously followed the Israelites throughout their journey. Once we have started the process of perceiving miracles, there really is no telling where it will end.

Even if we discount Paul's excessive enthusiasm, we are still left with two highly implausible narratives which no one has ever doubted were to be regarded as miraculous. But even here a non-miraculous origin for the stories can be found. Look at Psalm cxiv, which gives us a brief poetic description of the events of the Exodus; it concludes:

> Tremble, O earth, at the presence of the LORD,

at the presence of the God of Jacob,
who turns the rock into a pool of water,
the flint into a spring of water.
   (Psalm cxiv.7-8)

This could easily be, and originally almost certainly was, a description of a volcano spewing out lava. The fact that it quickly solidified into rock made it clear, even to the primitive mind of early Israel, that lava was essentially a form of molten rock. It was later, probably priestly, minds who saw the possibility of turning the imagery into a purely miraculous form, and simply couldn't resist; or just possibly they genuinely misunderstood what the text of Psalm cxiv was saying.

It is tempting to think that belief in miracles as a contravention of natural processes is characteristic of primitive thought, while more sophisticated minds (like that, for instance, of George Bernard Shaw) would prefer to see them rather as being manifested in purely natural processes; but the actual evidence points to the opposite conclusion. It is the primitive mind that is happy to see the hand of God at work in what to the rest of us are simply very lucky, or possibly very unlucky, incidents that have a perfectly natural explanation; and, on the contrary, it is the sophisticated mind which insists that, if God's activity is to be discerned, there must be a radical discontinuity between events which have a natural explanation – and are therefore not miraculous – and events which cannot possibly be explained in terms of natural causes, and therefore truly are miraculous.

I agree probably with all my hearers that descriptions of such miraculous events cannot possibly be true; at the same time, and probably to the disappointment of most of you – perhaps even to the anger of some – I confess I have no time for a religion that does not contain such miracles, not merely as an element, but even as the overridingly important element in its (for want of a better word) mythology.

It is likely that most of us would like to think of ourselves as in the van-guard of progressive thought, and are waiting for 'mainstream' religion to catch up with the approach to religious belief that MCU has long advocated. From some points of view this may be justified. Openly-stated disbelief in the Virgin Birth, for instance, or in the Bodily Resurrection, though still widely disapproved of, are no longer thought of as automatic disqualification for professing Christianity, or even perhaps wishing to be ordained, whereas fifty years ago they certainly would have been. There are those who still want to insist they are, but cannot for the moment muster support to enforce their view. But I would stress, this is for the moment; we cannot be sure that our position will always hold.

I would strongly warn against arguing it is the advance of science which has established the present position. This is only partially true. Principally, it is the sense of ease and prosperity which, increasingly since the Second World War, the cheap and abundant supply of oil has created which has much more to do with our very relaxed attitude to such things as belief and orthodoxy; when that comes to an end, as seems now to be in the very process of happening, it is likely that anxiety will increase, and with it will increase the demand for religious certainty and for the suppression of those views which appear to undermine it. Secondly, perhaps surprisingly to some of us, it is not chiefly scientists who cannot accept the reality of miracles. In America, though no doubt there still are many scientists who reject all talk of miracles on the grounds that belief in them is rendered impossible by our understanding of how the world actually works, and this understanding is amply vindicated by their proven ability to manipulate that world to human advantage, increasingly on the other hand there is no lack of scientists who insist that they have no difficulty at all in believing the truth of miracles, in particular the miracles of the Bible. In many cases I doubt their honesty, but it is often impossible to doubt their competence. The ones who never can accept the reality of miracles are, surprisingly, histo-rians. One of their primary tasks in interpreting the record is to be able to evaluate the worth of the documents which contain it. One of the first things they look for is accounts of miracles, and whenever they find them, they immediately conclude that the document is of limited value as a historical record. Stories of the resurrection are no exception to this rule.

When Paul tried to preach Christianity to the Areopagites, he assured them:

The times of ignorance God overlooked, but now he commands all men everywhere to repent, because he has fixed a day on which he will judge the world in righteousness by a man whom he has appointed, and of this he has given assurance by raising him from the dead.
(Acts xvii.30-31)

At that suggestion, of course, they all burst out laughing. The historian may doubt whether the episode of Paul preaching to the philosophers of Athens has any basis in history, but even if it hasn't, the point it illustrates is valid: in the first century AD the whole of the educated public would have been as immediately scornful of the idea of someone rising from the dead as we are told the Areopagites were; by the fifth century, if any Athenian still doubted the truth of the resurrection, he would have been well-advised to keep it to himself.

We still tell ourselves we are the vanguard of liberated scien-tific thought; but the truth is we are the tail-end of a Renaissance tradition in education which over the last thirty years has been systematically destroyed. When I was at school fifty years ago, it was taken for granted that a wide familiarity with, and a serious understanding of, the great tradition of the humanities in European thought was an essential ingredient – perhaps *the* essential ingredient – in all education. It was under threat to some extent even in those days; there were already those insisting that most of it was an utter waste of time, that scientific knowledge was the only thing that really counted any longer, that the humanities – like words generally – buttered no parsnips; and it was far more important that school-leavers should be qualified to earn their living than to be able to give themselves airs of being educated like gentlemen. In those days a lot of us could still laugh all that off as the bluster of techno-logical cranks. The dreadful appearance of the word 'elitist' as a pejorative in the seventies was the first indication that they were beginning to win the battle.

Other times, other customs. I was educated to the belief, as I suspect were most my of readers, that the worth of an idea was established by its ability to stand up to scrutiny and criticism. Since our day a generation has grown up which has no time for this idea at all, chiefly perhaps because it neglected to acquire the techniques of scrutiny and criticism which are necessary for the purpose. To this generation the worth of an idea, like that of any other commodity, is established by its ability to perform in the market place. Belief in miracles, belief generally, performs very well in the market place; skepticism on the other hand, and particularly those religions which encourage it, do not. Therefore belief in miracles is a worthwhile idea, while skepticism about them is not; and this seems to be true as much for unbelievers as for believers. The unbelieving community, particularly the upwardly mobile, seems to be saying to itself, 'Even though I am not a believer, and for the time being have no use for religion, should the day ever come when I needed it, I would plump for a real religion that has miracles and similar impossibilities in it rather for than for wishy-washy liberalism.'

Can I illustrate the point with yet another biblical excerpt:

Then Moses answered, 'But behold, they will not believe me or listen to my voice, for they will say, 'The LORD did not appear to you." The LORD said to him, 'What is that in your hand?' He said, 'A rod.' And he said, 'Cast it on the ground.' So he cast it on the ground, and it became a serpent; and Moses fled from it. But the LORD said to Moses, 'Put out your hand, and take it by the tail' – so he put out his hand and caught it, and it became a rod in his hand – 'that they may believe that the LORD, the God of their fathers, the God of Abraham, the God of Isaac, and the God of Jacob, has appeared to you.' Again, the LORD said to him, 'Put your hand into your bosom.' And he put his hand into his bosom; and when he took it out, behold, his hand was leprous, as white as snow. Then God said, 'Put your hand back in your bosom.' So he put his hand back into his bosom; and when he took it out, behold, it was restored like the rest of his flesh. 'If they will not believe you,' God said, 'or heed the first sign, they may believe the latter sign. If they will not believe even these two signs or heed your voice, you shall take some water from the Nile and pour it upon the dry ground; and the water which you shall take from the Nile will become blood upon the dry ground.'

(Exodus iv.1-9)

I presume all my readers take it for granted that these stories are untrue; it is entirely because we assume they are untrue, and we note the connection with religion, that we conclude they are miracles. Traditionalists, while arriving at this very same conclusion by very much the same means, nevertheless insist that they believe them. I have no wish to accuse them of insincerity, but I am bound to note that here they use the word 'believe' in a very different way than I do, and in a way that I'm not at all sure I understand. If I say I believe something, and I come across someone else who says they don't, this doesn't usually worry me. If I think it worthwhile, if I guess that my hearer has sufficient intelligence to follow the argument, I will set out the reasons why I do believe. He may well not be convinced; but once again, that does not worry me. He may offer counter-arguments of his own; but it is unlikely he will change my mind. Though in youth this did occasionally happen, at my age I am far too comfortable with the way I now think to be anything but very reluctant to question it. Arguments generally prevail, not by converting the opposition but by being persisted in until the opposition eventually dies. When you are arguing, your real audience should be, not the person you are talking to, but the bystander or overhearer. If they judge that you have won, then you have; your actual opponent is unlikely to admit it even if he feels it. But to return to the matter in hand.

All this normally takes place without any kind of agony or distress. But when we come to deal with the belief of the traditional believer, we are usually confronted with an immediate agony. The aim of his response is not to convince you of the truth of the belief, but to make you ashamed of doubting it: 'If you don't believe that, you're not a Christian.' Or, if that seems feeble and ineffective, then to frighten you – if not to assent, then at least to silence: 'If you don't believe it, you will burn in hell.' (The traditional arguments for religion, it seems, are still the best!) What this agony and distress tells us is that, when it comes to things like miracles, it is clear that the believers are just as aware of the improbability of what they profess to believe as are the rest of us. To say this is admittedly to approach the ultimate discourtesy of telling someone else what they really think as distinct from what they say they think; but it is hard to see any other explanation for what we observe. There appears to be far more agreement between belief and skepticism than the believer is willing to admit. His determination to suppress in himself those doubts which the rest of us freely acknowledge, and find no difficulty with, is precisely what he calls his faith.

Note, though, that this is not what the New Testament usually means by faith, which is something much more like a genuine moral quality. If we take Hebrews xi as the *locus classicus* for the definition of faith, then although faith still refers to impossibilities, the important point is that they are future impossibilities. The author, it is true, gives many examples from the past; but in every case the person involved rejects what the present world has to offer in favour of a new and better world which as yet does not exist:

> If they had been thinking of that land from which they had gone out, they would have had an opportunity to return. But as it is, they desire a better country, that is, a heavenly one. Therefore God is not ashamed to be called their God, for he has prepared for them a city.
> (Hebrews xi.15-16)

The 'promises of God', which according to the author of this document, are the true object of faith, are promises which in the here-and-now appear to be incapable of fulfillment; the moral quality of faith, however, is undeterred, and is determined to live now the kind of life that is contained in those promises, and by doing so brings forward their fulfillment. If I could quote from another document hinting at the same sort of thing:

> Since all these things [i.e. *the world about us*] are thus to be dissolved, what sort of persons ought you to be in lives of holiness and godliness, waiting for *and hastening* the coming of the day of God....
> (II Peter iii.11-12a)

What could be more reasonable than faith in this sense, and what more implausible and apparently useless than faith in the usual sense?; and yet, as we have seen, those that feel they need faith overwhelmingly plump for the latter and reject the former as rarefied and over-intellectual. Can we fathom why this should be so?

Those looking for faith are above all looking for something most of us here will immediately dismiss as an impossibility: certainty. We take it for granted that there is no such thing, that those that think they have found it are deceiving themselves, that many of those claiming to offer it are deliberate charlatans and liars. We preach the word in vain: those who tend to agree with us dismiss religion altogether, and everything to do with it; those who want religion can see no point in it unless it claims to offer certainty; and they recognize that offer of certainty precisely in belief in or, even better, performance of miracles. 'O set me up upon a rock that is higher than I,' cries the Psalmist, and that is precisely what miracles do for those who believe in them.

In the excerpt I quoted from Exodus iv Moses is instructed to perform his miracles on the grounds that, if he simply comes to the Israelites with a message of deliverance alone, his hearers will not believe him. It is the miracles which will prove that God has really sent him and, even more to the point, it is the miracles, far more than the mere message, which will convince the hearers that God is indeed about to deliver them. That is why the Israelites respond as they do:

> Then Moses and Aaron went and gathered together all the elders of the people of Israel. And Aaron spoke all the words which the LORD had spoken to Moses, and did the signs in the sight of the people. And the people believed; and when they heard that the LORD had visited the people of Israel and that he had seen their affliction, they bowed their heads and worshiped.
> (Exodus iv.30-31)

It begins to be clear why so many of us no longer believe in miracles: we feel we have no need of the kind of deliverance that miracles seem to promise. Our lives on the whole are easy; miracles are for those that the world treats harshly. It is significant that in Europe, where standards of welfare provided by the state are generally high, interest in religion tends to be low – and particularly in Scandinavia, where welfare provision tends to be higher than elsewhere, and interest in religion correspondingly lower. In America on the other hand – despite its wealth – welfare provision is meager in comparison, resulting in an intensity of need for religious support and consolation. There is nothing like anxiety for directing thoughts heaven-ward; and correspondingly, there is nothing like ease and satisfaction for banishing all thoughts of God. Jeshurun waxed fat – we are told in Deuteronomy xxxii.15 – and kicked.

There remains one loose end that needs tying up before I leave the theme. You will remember that I earlier said I had no time for any religion that did not have miracles as an important element in its mythology. Since throughout this talk I have insisted I do not admit that any miracle story can ever be true, this may now seem to some of you as a rather perverse stance to adopt; so let me try and explain it. We are conscious, or should I say the educated mind is conscious, of living life principally in two spheres: (a) that of the world of nature and (b) that of the forces of history. Christianity, here basing itself closely on biblical doctrine, insists that both these things are manifestations of a divine providence: nature as the consequence of God's initial act of creation, history as the sphere in which he operates to bring about man's obedience to his will. It would be overbold nowadays to insist that all scientists reject that view of nature; I will content myself with saying I accept the view of those scientists who make that rejection, acknowledging that I am relying on their expertise to justify my view, since I have none to call on of my own. In the sphere of history I believe I can confidently maintain there are no serious historians willing to accept the traditional Christian view; and it seems to me that study of the Bible will itself go a long way to vindicate their view. There is a great deal of apparently historical writing in the Bible, but almost all of it very obviously and very seriously distorted. The reason for this distortion is precisely the insistence that history is the sphere of God's activity; the authors repeatedly relate stories which we judge cannot be true, repeatedly offer explanations of events which do not convince, and can often enough actually be seen making comments or altering details which they do not care for in order to maintain this orthodoxy of God's direct control over human history. It is for reasons such as these that I take it for granted that we live in a world which has no detectable purpose nor meaning.

That is the world we really live in; but we, on the contrary, are necessarily and incurably creatures of purpose and meaning, and we simply cannot live in such a world. The task of religion – and this is what all religions seem to me to be about – is to reinterpret that world, so that it now appears to have purpose and meaning. I realize this idea of merely apparent purpose and meaning will not satisfy most people; but for me it has to be enough because there does not seem to be anything more available. Religion therefore *has to be* unreal; if it were real, it would itself be a part of that meaningless and purposeless world we are hoping it will deliver us from. The radical discontinuity between the real world and the religious view of it, which (as we have seen) has always been a feature of it almost to our own day, is of its very essence; when we try to dispense with it, we find ourselves dispensing with religion altogether. My guess is that this is one of the most important factors in the catastrophic decline in religious observance in our own day. When they took the decision back in the sixties to make religion more relevant to contemporary society, the practical consequence of what they were doing was precisely to get rid of this discontinuity – which they have been only too successful in doing.

A critical feature of Christian religious observance for me is Holy Week. Fifty years ago the ceremonies proper to this occasion were elaborate, intense and uplifting; but if one compared them with the original events, they were also highly unreal. Nowadays the whole emphasis of the observance is precisely on what those original events were like; the ceremonies accordingly are simple, low-key and deflating. The earlier ceremonies were attended by large numbers of rapt participants; the newer ones by mere handfuls of the dutiful and the conscientious. That to me is a paradigm for what, in the whole sphere of religion, has gone seriously and drastically wrong.

Honesty and Charity
in the Church of England

And one of the scribes came up and heard them disputing with one another, and seeing that he answered them well, asked him, 'Which commandment is the first of all? Jesus answered, 'The first is, 'Hear, O Israel: The Lord our God, the Lord is one; and you shall love the Lord your God with all you heart, and with all your soul, and with all your mind, and with all your strength.' The second is this, 'You shall love your neighbour as yourself.' There is no other commandment greater than these.'
(Mark xii.26-31)

There are, or ought to be, just two basic principles of the Christian religion: the first is an absolute commitment to truth and candour, and the second no less a commitment to the well-being of those around you. If you want that in two simple words, they are 'honesty' and 'charity', neither of which can the historic Church claim to have exemplified, and especially in the matter of what it is pleased to call 'church discipline'. As you know, it is only by the tiniest of margins that a proposal to reintroduce what are to all intents heresy trials has just been defeated. As the junky cannot live without his fix of heroin, so there is a certain kind of Christian who cannot live without 'knowing where we stand', even though a very lengthy chapter of the New Testament – Hebrews chapter xi – makes it clear that faith consists precisely in being able to carry on even though we *don't* know where we stand. For the moment the two principle points on which such Christians are determined to 'know where we stand', as the debate itself and subsequent discussion make clear, are the strangely unconnected ones of belief in the virgin birth and continued enforcement of St Paul's condemnation of homosexuality. In connection with the second let me say at once I accept that the New Testament really does say what evangelicals say it says; that is to say, the New Testament (which on this topic in practice this means St Paul), even when 'rightly interpreted', unquestionably does condemn out of hand all the practical aspects of homosexuality, and it is dishonest to try and argue the contrary. Nevertheless it will be obvious that the first of these two points is highly relevant to Jesus' call for honesty, while the second is no less relevant to the call for charity. It cannot be denied that throughout history the Church has committed frequent and appalling offences against both these principles – beginning, indeed, with the example of the very text in which Jesus makes this call. Here is how the above continues in Mark's gospel:

> And the scribe said to him, 'You are right, Teacher; you have truly said that he is one, and there is no other but he; and to love him with all the heart, and with all the understanding, and with all the strength, and to love one's neighbor as oneself, is much more than all whole burnt offerings and sacrifices.' And when Jesus saw that he answered wisely, he said to him, 'You are not far from the kingdom of God.'
> (Mark xii.32-34)

In other words, Mark gives us an account of an entirely friendly and admiring exchange between Jesus and the scribe. This will not do for Matthew, who firstly insists that the scribe asked Jesus the question 'to test him' (Matthew xxii.35), and then suppresses the whole of the further conversation between Jesus and the scribe that we have just given. Matthew cannot allow that relations between Jesus and the religionists of his day could be anything but hostile, and deliberately distorts the testimony before him to convey that impression. Even while telling us that for Jesus the prime moral duties for any Christian are honesty and charity, he calmly and coldly offends against both.

When we protest about insistence on belief in the virgin birth, it should first of all be clear that what we are protesting about is not the belief itself but the insistence. No one has any objection to evangelical Christians not merely believing in the virgin birth but loudly proclaiming that belief – even, perhaps, insisting on its importance: it does after all, have a prominent place in the creeds. What one objects to is the eagerness they show first of all to silence their opponents or, failing that, eject them altogether. And here we should note a strange but frequent feature of all traditional Christian belief. Those who are determined to 'contend for the faith which was once for all delivered to the saints' seem to think that some kind of moral victory has been achieved if they can force those who they know disagree with them either to be silent or else to say they believe things which everyone knows that in fact they don't. It is this that we are not only entitled to resist but, as far as I am concerned, morally obliged to do.

The bishops generally, though some more than others, would dearly like to avoid any discussion of these questions altogether. This morning's papers (12th July) carry a plea from Dr Hope, Archbishop of York, that we should not let schism occur over the question of homosexuality, but should 'move on from the debate and concentrate on the Church's original task of converting the unbeliever.' The practical consequences of this doctrine are abhorrent. The peace that Dr Hope pleads for – and it is hard to believe he is unaware of this – can be achieved only on one condition: not merely that no further discussion of the issue of homosexuality take place, but that no change to what evangelicals consider to be existing practice should be permitted; principally that no one known to be homosexual should ever be ordained, and that any bishop found to be in breach of this regulation should be 'disciplined' (and oh how much better they feel, once they've been allowed to utter that salvific term!). No man who wants to be considered even virtuous can possibly acquiesce to such wicked and oppressive demands:

Open your mouth for the dumb,
for the rights of all who are left desolate.
Open your mouth, judge righteously,
maintain the rights of the poor and needy.
(Proverbs xxxi.8-9)

They hope also to prevail by withholding 'contributions'; but any bishop worth his salt would refuse to accept such contributions in the first place: 'It is not lawful to put it into the treasury – it is the price of blood.'

However, before I go on to denounce this outrage against charity, I would like briefly to look at the outrage against honesty that underlies that other evangelical insistence, that all of us should state our clear belief in the virgin birth. This is but one example, but a particularly glaring one, of evangelical insistence that we should all at all times profess a belief in the literal truth of everything the Bible tells us. No one who is at all well-read in the Bible can honestly agree to the demand, and the topic chosen provides us with an excellent example of why this is so. It is true that chapter i of Matthew's gospel, and also chapter i of Luke's gospel, make the claim quite unambiguously; but even if there were no biblical material casting doubt on the claim, we still would not feel obliged to accept it, for a compelling reason which I shall give after I have discussed the specifically biblical difficulties.

The first point to make is that the claim that Jesus was born of a virgin is incompatible with any worthwhile claim that Jesus was directly descended from King David – note that descent through the female line is itself not what we traditionally mean by direct descent. Matthew's text shows quite clearly that he is well aware of the difficulty:

...and Eliud [was] the father of Eleazar, and Eleazar the father of Mathan, and Matthan the father of Jacob, and Jacob the father of Joseph, the husband of Mary, of whom Jesus was born, who is called Christ.

(Matthew 1.15-16)

That final attempt to reconcile the genealogy with the doctrine of the virgin birth has the effect of rendering the genealogy itself all but useless: we have a list of forty-two ancestors of Jesus 'father' Joseph, only to be told at the end of it that Joseph wasn't his father after all. But it can also be shown that Matthew has tinkered with the genealogy itself. The first 'fourteen genera-tions' accurately follow the Old Testament source, adding the brief genealogy at the end of the book of Ruth (iv.18-22) to that of Abraham, Isaac, Jacob and Judah. But when we look at the second group of fourteen generations, we cannot help noticing that Matthew has indulged in sleight of hand to boil down what was in fact rather more than the necessary fourteen generations, principally by confusing Ahaziah (who reigned very briefly in 841 BC) with Azariah, or Uzziah (who reigned from about 790 to 740 BC). As for the third group of fourteen generations, we have nothing to check it against, but it is more than probable that the entire list of names is fictional.

But this is only the least of the difficulties that anyone actually familiar with the Bible is going to have with the virgin birth. Matthew quotes Isaiah vii.14 as a prophecy of the event:

Behold, a virgin shall conceive and bear a son,
and his name shall be called Emmanuel.

But if you turn to the Hebrew text of Isaiah there is no mention of a virgin; what Matthew is actually quoting is a Septuagintal mistranslation of Isaiah's text, and Jews have been pointing this out to Christians throughout Christian history. It takes a very brazen impudence to insist that the error makes no difference to the 'truth' of the doctrine of the virgin birth.

Although the two chapters referred to above do insist that Jesus was born of a virgin, it is very remarkable that the claim is found nowhere else in the New Testament, not even anywhere else in the gospels themselves (unless John viii.41is a deliberately derisive reference to it). Paul's total silence on the subject would itself, for most of us, be a powerful indication that he had never heard the idea; but he seems to offer confirming evidence for that when he describes Jesus thus:

> But when the time had fully come, God sent forth his Son, born of a woman, born under the law…
> (Galatians iv.4)

It is, moreover, very clear from Acts that the earliest Christians knew nothing at all of Jesus' life prior to his baptism by John (Acts i.21-2, x.36-37, xiii.23-25), which is almost certainly why Mark's gospel – our earliest – begins with that event.

All these are difficulties raised by the biblical material itself, and all of them require an answer before anyone can be required to assent to the doctrine as any kind of obligation. But there is a non-biblical difficulty which makes it all but impossible to assent no matter what the Bible says, and it is this: Supposing it were true that Jesus actually was born of a virgin, how would we know that it was true? And simply to raise that very obvious question proves – *proves* – that the whole idea can only be a fiction. It is surely absurd to argue that there is some kind moral virtue in setting all our misgivings aside and in insisting on believing the doctrine regardless. Simple honesty, one of the two qualities which Jesus insisted were of overriding importance and the very foundation of the religion he was preaching, prevents us from accepting the idea without question.

The case is not so simple with regard to homosexuality since, as admitted above, despite the protests of the liberal tendency, conservatives and evangelicals claim no more than the truth when they insist that the Bible (in reality St Paul) utterly condemns all aspects of being homosexual; he does not even sanction, for instance, the modern let-out that *being* homosexual is morally neutral, it is *acting* homosexually that is the unpardonable sin. The nearest you can get to that idea is Paul's otherwise mystifying admission:

> And to keep me from being too elated by the abundance of revelations, a thorn was given me in the flesh, a messenger of Satan, to harass me, to keep me from being too elated. Three times I besought the Lord about this, that it should leave me; but he said to me, 'My grace is sufficient for you, for my power is made perfect in weakness.'
> (II Corinthians xii.7-9a)

He does not make clear just what this 'thorn in the flesh' was, but many suspect (including myself) that Paul was aware that he himself was homosexual; though on the other hand one certainly cannot claim to be able to deduce this from the actual text.

Granted, then, that everything said about homosexuality in the New Testament condemns it, can one avoid the conservative evangelical position on the subject? But just as the non-biblical objection to the doctrine of the virgin birth will for most people be the clincher, so here it is non-biblical considerations that convince, not merely many Christians, but almost all decent-minded human beings to reject the St Paul's position. Paul, after all, says many hard things about women in his epistles (though admittedly nowhere near as hard as what he says about homosexuals), which the church has traditionally embraced with enthusiasm; but nowadays secular society finds his attitude pointlessly oppressive and prejudiced, and goes a long way in enforcing what it believes to be a juster and fairer approach even on Christians – and, to be fair, many evangelicals accept modern ideas on the subject in preference to those of the New Testament. But a much more graphic example of the same preference is provided by the church's attitude to Jews. Traditionally this has been not merely hostile but often quite frankly murderous; we find it abhorrent now, but there is no denying that the New Testament provides no lack of support for it, particularly of course in the following:

> So when Pilate saw that he was gaining nothing, but rather that a riot was beginning, he took water and washed his hands before the crowd, saying, 'I am innocent of this man's blood; see to it yourselves.' And all the people answered, 'His blood be on us and on our children!'
> (Matthew xxvii.24-25)

Once again, no matter what the New Testament says we know that this is morally wrong – even conservative evangelicals know it. And the same is true of homosexuality. The church used to rejoice in oppressing Jews; that is now illegal, and rightly so. It used also to give women a pretty hard time, and the same is true. It is now time that homosexuals benefitted from the same change of heart that Christians have at last adopted towards those other two groups.

An Address to the American House of Bishops

> You were running well; who hindered you from obeying the truth? This persuasion is not from him who called you.
> (Galatians v.7-8.)

I could have chosen any number of texts from the epistle to the Galatians which directly speak to the present crisis, and many of them will in fact appear as this address proceeds. But the above is particularly appropriate to the event that has called this forth, namely the assent, even though grudgingly – perhaps even insincerely (I hope insincerely) – given after a long and unequal struggle against the now notorious *Windsor Report*. The occasion of that report was the consecration of the Rt Revd Gene Robinson to be Bishop of New Hampshire. Did you do well to approve, even to participate, in that consecration? If you did, and let me assure you that your courage in following the promptings of your hearts, and defying the bigotry of those who seem to have very little heart at all, was an inspiration to many of us in all parts of the Communion, even where (as here in England) the hierarchy seem determined to sacrifice not only moral principles but actual human beings to the dubious cause of maintaining the 'unity' of the Anglican Communion at all costs – if you did well, then what was the point of accepting under any circumstances a document that insists you acted wrongly?

But first let us examine the issue that is the cause of the division. Some evangelicals will no doubt be scandalized that I have chosen a text from the writings of Paul as a basis for an attack on an idea that Paul himself insisted on, namely that homosexuality is in all its forms a sinful activity. I know there are liberals who deny this, but I have no hesitation in admitting that on this point they are wrong, and that the current evangelical interpretation of Paul's view is, as far as I am concerned, accurate. I can see no specific reference in Paul's writings to boy prostitution on the one hand, nor on the other to faithful and loving same-sex relations. The *malakoi* of I Corinthians vi.9 quite possibly often were boy prostitutes, but in fact the passive partner in most homosexual couplings in those days would most likely have been a slave-boy who had absolutely no say in what was happening to him; but Paul seems uninterested in the details and condemns them all out of hand any way – not just the person making use of the *malakos*, but the actual passive partner himself. On the other hand, it is true that the New Testament nowhere condemns faithful and loving same-sex relationships, but only because it nowhere mentions them; the evidence suggests that such an idea had simply never occurred. Paul's condemnation of homosexuality is a clear, unambiguous, above all a *blanket* condemnation; that is the background against which the argument must take place.

So then evangelicals are right? If we are to be faithful to biblical ethics, we must accept, proclaim, even enforce, Paul's condemnation? Such is the argument; but we ought to note that we – all of us – even evangelicals – perhaps especially evangelicals – have already abandoned the position in connection with another Pauline pronouncement. There are about as many passages about slavery in the New Testament as there are about homosexuality; they too are clear, unambiguous and all-embracing, and they justify the practice. But we all decided two hundred years ago that, if he was not actually mistaken on the subject, Paul's views were of limited value and, because of the unjust and cruel oppression that insistence on his views occasioned, those views must be set aside and the victims of that oppression liberated. And that is exactly the position we are now arguing for in connection with homosexuality. It is no good evangelicals protesting that such an argument flies in the face of the clear position of scripture. It does indeed, but evangelicals themselves have already agreed to such a procedure in the one case, and it is now time for them to do the same in the other – and for the same reason: namely that strict adherence to the scriptural position has resulted in an unjust and cruel oppression.

If it happens that Paul is against us on the question of homosexuality, he is nevertheless very much on our side on another aspect of the present controversy, namely the hostility of conservative minds to the promoters of change and innovation; and nowhere more so than in his letter to the Galatians, which is wholly devoted to just that topic. The last thing he would recommend in such a situation is accommodation of the kind that the Archbishop of Canterbury has insistently pressed for and you American bishops have belatedly agreed to. On the contrary, when confronted with 'false brethren secretly brought in, who slipped in to spy out our freedom which we have in Christ Jesus, that they might bring us in to bondage' he tells us that 'to them we did not yield submission even for a moment, that the truth of the gospel might be preserved for you.' Defiance, and not concession, should have been your watchword in greeting our recent ambassador to you, the Bishop of Durham. And even more perhaps to the Archbishop of Canterbury himself. Dr Williams is not a wicked man, but he has proved to be a spineless one, and his fearless commitment to cowardice has brought the Communion to the brink of a disaster which now probably cannot be averted. No more than Peter at Antioch can he avoid the charge of deliberate and conscious insincerity. Rowan Williams as Archbishop of Wales was precisely the kind of bishop that Rowan Williams as Archbishop of Canterbury is now trying to browbeat into submission. Your reaction to him should be the same as Paul's reaction to Peter's manifest dishonesty and insincerity. 'For before certain men came from James, he ate with Gentiles; but when they came he drew back and separated himself, fearing the circumcision party. And with him the rest of the Jews acted insincerely, so that even Barnabas was carried away.' Not therefore by accommodation. Not by agreeing to Peter's insistence that we cannot afford to alienate the 'circumcision party'? On the contrary, Paul 'opposed him to his face, because he stood condemned.' And that is what you should have done – nor is it too late to do it now. Those of you who are convinced of the utter wrongheadedness of the whole enterprise which resulted in *The Windsor Report* must surely now stand up and say so, not quietly among yourselves so as not to rock the boat, but openly and vehemently speak boldly as they ought to speak. The damage to the Anglican Communion which so many of you seem to fear has in fact already been done, so that the very notion of such a Communion has now been rendered morally bankrupt by the shamelessness of the compromises of principle that were made to preserve it.

In Christ Jesus, Paul assures us, we are all sons of God through faith. He goes on to list pairs of distinctions which no longer have any force: 'For as many of you as were baptized into Christ have put on Christ. There is neither Jew nor Greek, there is neither slave nor free, there is neither male nor female...' But he has left out the last pairing surely; the list cries out to be completed with, 'There is neither straight nor gay'. Our modern view of homosexuality as a wholly natural condition, as much a part of nature as heterosexuality, undoubtedly contradicts the biblical view, and in particular the Pauline view. There are those for whom this automatically means that the Bible must be right, and therefore we must be wrong. And yet they eat black pudding without a qualm, though we are assured – by the New Testament as well as the Old (Acts xv.29, xxi.25) – that this is one of the worst sins you can possibly commit. Their wives and daughters happily go to church – oh horror! – without any covering for their heads (I Corinthians xi.2-16, one of the longest continuous arguments in the whole of Paul's writings). They utterly ignore Jesus' unambiguous and repeated demand that his disciples abandon all family ties and all property, and follow him as a beggar on the road. I do not think they are at fault on any of these points, but it does render ludicrous their contention that they have to insist on the condemnation of homosexuals because it is scriptural. Where the scriptural shoe pinches their own feet they happily remove it; they insist it must be worn only where it pinches other people.

If we look again at the contrasting pairs listed above, the Christian tradition has a very poor record in connection with every one of them. It *has* discriminated between Jews and its own non-Jewish cultural background; it *has* discriminated between the slave and the free; and it has certainly discriminated until very recent times, and even yet in large parts of the Anglican Communion, between male and female. You yourselves have an excellent record on remedying this last injustice, and quite a good one on removing the injustices suffered by homosexuals. Your acceptance of *The Windsor Report* is a step backward. I hope I can persuade at least some of you to step forward again, either as a united body or, if that is not for the moment possible, then for those of you who see the wrong that has recently been done to have the courage to stand up as individuals and protest against it. It is likely that your recent decision about the report was a cosmetic exercise only, and that many, probably most, of you are in your own minds opposed to it and do not intend to let it have much influence on your actual practice. Yet even this is nevertheless to strengthen your opponents, and to deny to your friends in other churches what is beginning to look like their only hope and comfort. And there is in any case a presumption in matters of open debate (as distinct from cynical politics, of which we have all become victims in recent years) in favour of at all times saying what you mean and meaning what you say.

'For freedom Christ has set us free; stand fast therefore, and do not submit again to a yoke of slavery.' What you have been doing is right, and those who are protesting against you, trying to inhibit you and, if that fails, to exclude you, are wrong. You are being asked to call it sincerity, and thus to give them no offense; but call it by what is often and evidently its right name – self-indulgent peevishness – and you are under an obligation to resist them: they bind heavy burdens, hard to bear, and lay them on men's shoulders, but they themselves will not move them with their finger. *The Windsor Report* presents itself as an attempt to preserve the unity of the Anglican Communion. Let me remind you that all the great crimes of Christianity have been perpetrated in the name of preserving – or, if necessary, imposing – unity, and *The Windsor Report* is no different in that respect. They make much of you, but for no good purpose; they want to shut you out so that you may make much of them.

'…it is written that Abraham had two sons, one by a slave and one by a free woman. But the son of the slave was born according to the flesh, the son of the free woman through promise. Now we, brethren, like Isaac, are children of promise. But as at that time he who was born according to the flesh persecuted him who was born according to the Spirit, so it is now. But what does the scripture say? "Cast out the slave and her son; for the son of the slave shall not inherit with the son of the free woman." So, brethren, we are not children of the slave, but of the free woman.' Amen – so let it be.

Compromise and Schism

But when Cephas came to Antioch I opposed him to his face, because he stood condemned. For before certain men came from James, he ate with the Gentiles; but when they came he drew back and separated himself, fearing the circumcision party. And with him the rest of the Jews acted insincerely, so that even Barnabas was carried away by their insincerity. But when I saw that they were not straightforward about the truth of the gospel, I said to Cephas before them all, 'If you, though a Jew, live like a Gentile and not a Jew, how can you compel the Gentiles to live like Jews? We ourselves, who are Jews by birth and not Gentile sinners...

(Galatians ii.11-15)

I was required as a boy to read Bunyan's *Pilgrim's Progress*, and though now – fifty odd years later – the memory of its contents is fading, I seem to remember there was this character in it called 'Mr Facing Both Ways', and also that Bunyan himself had a low opinion of him. The following report appeared in today's *Telegraph* (30th July 2008):

In an emotional plea for peace at the Lambeth Conference, Dr Rowan Williams... warned liberals that their actions were felt as a 'body blow' by some, and told conservatives who had defected from their churches in protest that their reaction 'pours scorn' on the Church's legitimacy.

It would not be fair to complain that his Grace tries to avoid taking sides in the controversy; but referees have to make decisions, and we are entitled to complain of the way he appears desperate to avoid doing even that. Elijah's standpoint was, *'How long will you go limping with two different opinions? If the* LORD *is*

God, follow him; but if Baal, then follow him (I Kings xviii.21b)'.
Rowan takes the opposite view: if we decide for the LORD, alas,
the Baal worshipers will feel it as a 'body blow'; so both sides
must avoid taking any kind of stand, because to do so would
cause pain to their opponents.

In Paul's time it is likely the majority of almost any Christian
congregation were converted Jews; and we can tell, particularly
from what Paul writes to the congregation at Rome, that a lot of
these converted Jews (who probably, by the way, did not even
see themselves as converts) had doubts, even severe doubts,
even in some cases were openly hostile to the idea, that Gentiles
had any place in a Christian congregation. The truth of their
claim that Jews were acceptable to God was proved by the fact
– which no one, not even Paul himself, denied – that God's
divinely appointed law had been delivered to the Jewish nation,
and not to anyone else. Only Jews, therefore, had the right to
appropriate God's promises. Gentiles might (just possibly) be
allowed in if they converted to Judaism first; but there were
probably some Jews who had doubts even about that,

> And thought the Church in danger was
> By such prevarication.

It is unlikely that Peter himself was of that opinion in view of
the fact it was he who first of any had dared not only to preach
the gospel to a group of Gentiles, but even worse to eat with
them, and even worse than that to baptize them. His moral
failing – and Paul was quite right to identify it as such – was to
seem to acquiesce in the conservative view, to treat Gentiles as
not quite the real thing, in order to avoid giving offence to
such conservatives. The fault was all the greater because (as a
consequence of the Cornelius incident) it was known that he
himself did not in fact accept the conservative point of view at
all.

So with Rowan. One of his first acts as Archbishop of Canterbury was to approve the Bishop of Oxford's recommendation that Canon Jeffrey John – an admitted homosexual in an apparently stable relationship – should be the next Bishop of Reading. There was an immediate outcry from the moral tendency – the so-called Anglican Mainstream, the Evangelical Council and so forth – protesting against the appointment of a conspicuous sinner to such a post. (Note that even Paul himself, in the passage quoted above, lets slip the notion that Gentiles are automatically to be thought of as 'sinners'.) What was Rowan's reaction? With the same fearless cowardice that he has manifested throughout his time in office – the same kind of cowardice that Peter showed at Antioch – without apology he immediately backed down. Can he wonder if ever since both sides in the debate have increasingly regarded him as an irrelevance?

It is easy to call for compromise, and certainly all liberals are agreed on the general need for it. But in this particular instance, why does he not specify what particular compromises are called for? If he were to do that (and probably he is aware of this, which is why he doesn't), it would be immediately apparent how shabby and unprincipled – how incompatible with what Paul calls 'the truth of the gospel' – are the compromises he has in mind. Please, please, please, for instance, abandon the notion that the ordination (not to speak of the consecration) of homosexuals is legitimate; that traditional Protestant orthodoxy can be questioned; that the Bible is anything other than a precise and detailed rule-book whose every requirement is to be followed to the letter. If not these, then what? But if these, then how does he reconcile them with his own every pronouncement prior to becoming Archbishop of Canterbury? He could of course boast (were he given to boasting) that he himself has compromised on every one of them; that, for most of us, is the trouble.

And what compromises does he require of the other side? Once again he does not specify, but there is one obvious compromise which, if accepted, would enable all of us to carry on without falling out. No one has ever tried to silence conservative evangelicals; no one has ever suggested it; no one even seems to desire it. The whole quarrel is over their obvious desire to silence all who disagree with them. Yes, if they wish to insist that all forms of homosexuality are sinful – which is unquestionably the view of Paul in the New Testament – I doubt if anyone is going to question their right to say so loudly and clearly; but if they have that right, then those who disagree with them have the same right. And if they could be persuaded that such people are as sincere as they, as well-intentioned as they, as eager for morality as they; and that such disagreements do not of themselves render it impossible for them both to worship with their opponents and to work with them – then on the basis of such a compromise we will all of us be able to continue.

Those who attended GAFCON are certainly justified in their belief that their aims and outlook are much closer to traditional Christianity than those of the rest of us. But is anyone going to argue that the history of the Christian Church is without blemish? The desire for certainty, the need for precision, the demand for orthodoxy – all of these have been the source of nothing but quarreling. And it is easy to see why. There is no intellectually honest way of achieving any of them; they are all of them the result, not of enquiry or observation, but quite simply of acts of legislation: not, 'This is what is true', but, 'This is what we must all say is true'. The second is clearly a very different kind of proposition from the first, and clearly rather sinister in comparison.

The overriding aim of Rowan's endeavours has always been to prevent schism – and, to be fair, he has had a surprising degree of success in achieving it. But should that really be the aim? – because, as Paul noted, the 'truth of the gospel' is surely more important than such an aim, and tends to be betrayed by those pursuing it. In Paul's day the majority of Christians were Jews;

fifty years later this was no longer the case. Why? Because Paul had won the argument, and those who found themselves unable to accept it had simply left; had that not happened, Christianity would probably be a minor sect within Judaism to this day. To take an example nearer home, the Lambeth Conference of ten years ago passed a resolution on the subject of homosexuality abhorrent to liberal minds – and known to be. Were the bishops worried that such a resolution would cause a schism? On the contrary, that's exactly what they were hoping for: that liberals would take offense at it and leave. Ten years ago, under the leadership of Dr Carey, conservative evangelicals were convinced that for all practical purposes they were the Anglican Communion. Rowan clearly inherited that view, and in his early years all his actions seem to have been dictated by it. More recently it has become clear they are in fact a minority, and Rowan seems to be modifying his stance in the light of that realization. By all means reassure them that they have a place, but remind them at the same time they do not rule; we can all perfectly well get on together on the basis of that compromise. And those who simply cannot accept such a compromise, like the Christian Jews of Paul's day, will quietly drift away. This is not a tragedy; it is simply evolution.

As long as the overriding aim continues to be the avoidance of schism, the row will rumble on. Those opposed to innovation will always be able to prevent it by threatening schism if innovation is allowed. They will insistently demand concessions to their point of view, and in Rowan's early years they openly boasted that they could make him do anything they asked of him. As the realization grew that their faction was less powerful than they initially believed, their demands – and even their complaints – have lessened in intensity. And the whole idea of GAFCON has turned out to be a miscalculation. The fact that they suffered a failure of nerve and drew back from a declaration of separateness has greatly weakened their bargaining power;

had they made such a declaration, on the other hand, it would have destroyed it altogether. They put themselves in a situation where they could only suffer loss. But Rowan shows no signs of being able to evaluate the situation; he still has the overriding aim of avoiding schism, which means he will be plagued by the threat of it for the whole of his time in office. In Paul's time the side that lost the argument simply drifted away and the controversy ceased; that is the only way such controversies ever cease. Allow both sides to freely speak their minds, prevent them from inhibiting their opponents, and history – not the Evangelical Alliance, but history – will eventually decide which of the two views is to prevail. And peace will then be restored.

An Open Letter to the Rt Revd
Tom Wright, Bishop of Durham

My Lord:

The trouble that you are in, and the trouble that the Church as a whole is in, has one overriding cause: some of the bishops, mostly of an evangelical persuasion, have deluded themselves into thinking they have much greater powers of coercion than in fact they have or are ever likely to have. It was never the belief of any of the participants in Lambeth 1.10 and the now notorious *Windsor Report* that they were in fact 'declaring the mind of the Church'; they were all well aware that the issue their pronouncements were dealing was highly contentious, and that the conclusion they were espousing was equally contentious. Their naïve hope was that these pronouncements would lead at first to silencing, later (if all went well) to extruding, all who disagreed with them. The bishops of the global south, for all I know, may be able in their own dioceses to carry on like this; the bishops of the Church of England are perfectly aware they can't, but seem embarrassed to admit it openly before other provinces of the Communion.

One is particularly irritated by the repeated, and largely meaningless, insistence on 'the authority of Scripture', as though it is and has always been the case that whatever Scripture says on any topic must be the unalterable rule for the Church for ever. Any passably educated person, which includes all the English bishops, knows that such a claim is bogus. Scripture prohibits lending money at interest; advancing capitalism forced the Church to change its mind on that in the early seventeenth century. Scripture is completely tolerant of the institution of slavery, giving instructions on how Christian slaves (Ephesians vi.5-9, Colossians iii.22-iv.1, Titus ii.9-10) of Christian masters (I

Timothy vi.1-2) are to conduct themselves; although there was fierce opposition to the change – even among Christians themselves – in the eighteenth century (and in America well into the nineteenth century), the Church as a whole came round to agreeing that the institution of slavery was incompatible with Christianity. And notably, of course, the Church has been forced to change its mind over the claim that the early chapters of Genesis give us a true and accurate account of how the world was made. It is noticeable that in every case it was the losing side of the argument which could justly claim that it took its stand on 'the authority of Scripture'.

In the present case it is perfectly true that liberals take a view of homosexuality which is incompatible with that of Scripture; there is nothing new, let alone reprehensible, in that – nor, in view of the history of all such controversies, does it indicate they are even likely eventually to lose the argument. On the contrary, it is their opponents who give every indication of being aware the argument is going against them; it is this that accounts for their frenzied and unreasoning reliance on 'the declared teaching of the Church'. Dr. Carey behaved as he did at Lambeth 1998, not in order to settle the question, but to try and preempt the possibility of an eventual settlement which he believed (almost certainly correctly) would be the opposite of the one he favored.

If one were to ask your lordship what it is that is inherently objectionable in homosexuality, how would you answer? All the assumptions (or, some would say, prejudices) which you could have relied on even thirty years ago have, in the intervening period, been taken away. It is no longer believed, for instance, that homosexuality is 'unnatural'. Indeed, the clergy themselves – even those most hotly opposed to the prevailing attitude of tolerance – seem to acknowledge that homosexuality is an inherent disposition; and once they admit that, whether they like it or not, they automatically admit that homosexuality occurs 'naturally'. All societies that have acted on the assumption that homosexuality can be completely accommodated, and that no dangers or disorders will normally arise as a result, have found in the event that their assumption was justified; it is only those groups in society that are determined to see homosexuality as threatening disruption and disorder – as, for instance, the Catholic Church – that still find it so. The only answer left to you is to insist that homosexuality is a sin on no other ground than that Scripture says it is; and even you can see that this is in fact no answer at all. Yes, Scripture does declare it to be abhorrent; no, this is not enough to make it so. 'Tend the flock of God that is your charge, not by constraint but willingly...not as domineering over those in your charge but being examples to the flock' (I Peter v.2-3). It is true the Christian Church has been reluctant to follow this advice; it is good advice nevertheless. Your lordship need only take it to heart for peace and brotherly affection to break out, not only in the diocese of Durham, but also in the Anglican Communion at large.

With sincere good wishes and a hope for your early repentance and amendment

DAVID BRUCE TAYLOR

Civil Partnerships – An Answer to the Bishop of Rochester's Answer

'You have heard that it was said to the men of old…But I say to you…' (Matthew v.21 and 22, 27 and 28, *see also* 31 and 32, 33 and 34, 38 and 39, 43 and 44).

The claims that conservative evangelicals make for the New Testament – that the text is directly given by God, and that its moral injunctions are an eternal, absolute and unchanging rule for human life at all times and everywhere – are just those that Jesus was rejecting for the Scriptures of his day, what we now call the Old Testament. Their doctrine was not evil, but it certainly was not absolute and unchanging; it could be improved upon, and needed to be. And if we are true followers of Jesus, what we find him doing in Matthew chapter v is what we need to do now *and will always need to do*: there is no such thing as an absolute and unchanging morality. A further lesson we need to learn is that institutional religion – because of its built-in tendency towards rigidity and regulation, and its excessive reluctance ever to adapt old rules to new situations – turns traditions that have their origin in an attempt to ease the lot of humanity into oppressive and tyrannical legalism (*see above all* Matthew chapter xxiii.) In his day, and in his view, the way observation of the Sabbath was interpreted by the clergy was the overriding example of this tyranny – provoking the outcry that 'The Sabbath was made for man, not man for the Sabbath' (Mark ii.27).

What the Sabbath was to the ancient Pharisee, it seems that marriage has become for the modern one. The trouble with the Civil Partnership Act, we are told, is that 'its ambiguity was not consistent with fundamental Christian teaching on marriage'. There will be – indeed, there are – many Christians who have no difficulty agreeing with that observation but who nevertheless consider the Act to be a very good thing. The Church, we are told, 'could have derogated [from the Act] on the grounds that the 'marriage-like' character... would be unacceptable to a substantial number of its members.' Once again, there is no quarreling with the observation itself; one objects to the unspoken conclusion that it is only the views of this 'substantial number' that really count; there is an equally 'substantial number' of Christians for whom the innovation is wholly acceptable – and even welcome. And there is an even more glaring omission earlier in the piece: 'It is widely recognized on all sides that people living together, for one reason or another, can face significant hardship and discrimination. For those in heterosexual relationships, one way to resolve these difficulties is to get married, but this is not possible where the cohabitees are of the same-sex or closely related to one another.' And how does it go on? You expect something like, 'For them I suggest ...', but if so you will be disappointed: the Bishop has no suggestions to make as regards a remedy for the hardships and discrimination that same-sex couples have to face, even though it is they, rather than heterosexual pairs, that exemplify the problem.

St Paul, of course, solved his personal dilemma (read whatever you like into that) by deciding to remain celibate, and most conservative evangelicals still see that as the only possible solution for homosexuals who also wish to be Christians. For the rest of us, the doctrine that if you are born queer you must accept that never in your whole life can you hope to experience the joy of sex is to be condemned, not principally because it is plainly unChristian, but principally because it is plainly mad. The Prayer Book lists 'the causes for which Matrimony was ordained' thus:

First, It was ordained for the procreation of children, to be brought up in the fear and nurture of the Lord, and to the praise of his holy name.

Secondly, It was ordained for a remedy against sin, and to avoid fornication; that such persons as have not the gift of continency might marry, and keep themselves undefiled members of Christ's body.

Thirdly, It was ordained for the mutual society, help, and comfort, that the one ought to have of the other, both in prosperity and adversity.

In the case of same-sex unions we will presume that the first of these does not apply; but the other two apply to homosexual unions just as much as to heterosexual ones. What provision is to be made for those (many) homosexuals that are well aware they 'have not the gift of continency'? Orthodoxy insists that the tradition supplies a remedy – marriage! Homosexual marriage? Of course not; such an abomination is prohibited by Scripture. The remedy is heterosexual marriage. But, we reply, there is abundant evidence that heterosexual marriage does not provide such a remedy for homosexuals. The only answer to that is a surly insistence that Scripture is God-given revelation and must be obeyed. We know what Jesus had to say to those who transformed the temple from a house of prayer into a den of thieves: what would he have to say to those who profess to be his followers, but yet – like the Pharisees of his own day – have transformed Scripture from a message of hope and deliverance into a monstrosity of unreason and oppression.

The Way Ahead after Dar es Salaam: A Letter to the American Bishops

Isn't it time to declare your independence? If America could respond with such outrage to the imagined tyranny of George III, is it sensible to submit like lambs to the real tyranny of the Primate's meeting at Dar es Salaam? They claimed to be discussing the future of the Communion, but one look at the document makes it clear they were *wholly* concerned with discussing you. Out of thirty-six paragraphs, only the first eight even pretend to be concerned with more general matters.

The two sticking-points the document identifies are the 1998 Lambeth Resolution 1.10, and the Windsor Report. Discussion throughout assumes there is an all-but-universal acceptance of both, whereas all the participants were certainly aware there is in fact a widespread rejection of both. The refusal even to hint at such a reality is what gives the document its hideous aura of deceit and menace. It reads not unlike the pronouncements that used to be issued by the Soviet Union: if you refuse to acknowledge reality, it is the same as if that reality does not exist.

When the Lambeth Resolution was first passed, those of us who rejected it were not particularly worried. There was no obligation to accept it, and no means of enforcing such an obligation if there had been. The Windsor Report began to change all that, and Dromantine, and now Dar es Salaam, were and are attempts to carry it further. The Anglican Communion that is revealed (admittedly only in prospect as yet, rather than in reality) is wholly different from the organization to which we all thought we belonged. The most obvious threat is to our hitherto assumed right to speak our mind; the frequent reference to the 'bonds of affection' (another double-speak redolent of the Soviet Union) actually means – quite unmistakably – bonds of constraint.

On Sunday 18th February, the day before the meeting started, the Primates traveled to Zanzibar to celebrate the Eucharist in the cathedral, which was built on the site of the old slave-market. I wonder what the epistle reading was. I know what it should have at any rate included:

> Let all who are under the yoke of slavery regard their masters as worthy of all honour, so that the name of God and the teaching may not be defamed. Those who have believing masters must not be disrespectful on the ground that they are brethren; rather they must serve all the better, since those who benefit by their service are believers and beloved. Teach and urge these duties.
>
> (I Timothy vi.1-2)

Clearly the Christian church has changed its mind considerably since those days. Those who campaigned for the abolition of slavery in the eighteenth century had to set aside the New Testament's unambiguous and repeated endorsement of slavery (Ephesians vi.5-8, Colossians iii.22-25), to the horror and dismay of those Christians who actually owned slaves, and who plausibly argued on the basis of the above texts that slavery could not possibly be inconsistent with the gospel. The campaigners nevertheless set all that aside, arguing that such texts had become a pretext for cruel and unjust oppression. In the same way, if some Christians today argue that, although it is true the New Testament condemns homosexuality, that too has become a pretext for oppression that is only a little less cruel and unjust, are they really doing anything unprecedented? Conservatives may not be persuaded, but can they claim justification for rejecting such a view out of hand, or refusing to even to talk to those who hold it.

And this points to the real issue of the debate, which is not specifically about homosexuality at all, but about the supposed right of some members of the communion to impose their views on all the rest. No one has ever suggested, nor are they suggesting now, that conservative views should be suppressed or excluded. What is at issue is whether conservatives can claim a right to silence or exclude their opponents. Dar es Salaam makes it clear they openly claim such a right, and that Dr Williams is ready – is *always* ready – to concede whatever demands they make.

We have the strange spectacle, in Britain at any rate, of the media, though overwhelmingly staffed by people holding views on this issue close to those advocated by liberals, nevertheless appearing in their comment to side with evangelicals, and to assume that in this – as in all previous rows between the two parties – it is the evangelicals who will carry the day. Journalists are not concerned with who is right and who is wrong. It's religion, isn't it! Questions of right and wrong, truth and falsehood simply do not apply. The reason for their stance is that evangelicals, when asked to state their views, use a tone of voice that is confident and challenging, while liberals, on the other hand, invariably sound diffident and apologetic. Liberals, if they wish to make a better impression on the general public, must learn to make the same assumption as evangelicals do that theirs is the real voice of truth.

And the first point on which to announce this change is on the meaning and proper use of scripture. In the Dar es Salaam statement, as in all previous ones, there is frequent reference to scripture and to the authority of scripture (but a total absence of any actual references to it!). Evangelicals assume – and sadly I think they may be right – that most liberals are not all that familiar with scripture, so that any reference to it immediately silences the opposition. Liberals give the impression (rarely more than that) that they do not accept the claims evangelicals make for what kind of book the Bible is and what kind of authority it should have, but they avoid making any precise claims of their own, and that is their big tactical mistake.

They should state openly, without apology or equivocation, that in their view the whole of Reformation theology is based on claims about scripture which are utterly implausible. Firstly it is not a rule book: Christians are perfectly entitled to have black pudding for breakfast, their wives are perfectly entitled to go to church bare-headed, and even to deliver the occasional sermon - all things which are prohibited by the New Testament, but that does not mean they are prohibited. And secondly it is not a revelation; Paul's views, in particular, are not necessarily those of God. God was not speaking directly through the mouth of Paul when Paul condemned homosexuality, any more than he was when Paul endorsed slavery. The Bible is a collection of ancient documents put together to be the basis of a value system. Treated that way it still works well – and it works even better when combined and contrasted with that other value system bequeathed by the ancient world, the pagan classics, which can also have a wonderfully cooling influence on the perfervid zeal that often results from attention to scripture alone.

Liberals like to live in the center of the modern world, which is another tactical mistake: the modern world is not convinced that it has any need of them. It is dubious also about any possible relevance of the ancient world; but that did have relevance in the past, so that (if only for historical reasons) it cannot entirely be neglected. Yet liberals do have a tendency to neglect it, or at least – which is just as bad – to give the impression that they do; some of the younger clergy scarcely conceal their real opinion that scripture is a load of unreadable old rubbish. Even if it were, if your opponents place great emphasis on it and appear to win the argument by doing so, it follows that you too must incorporate a knowledge of it into the debate. Just as your righteousness must exceed that of the scribes and Pharisees, so must your knowledge of scripture.

Now let us look at some of the detail of this latest report. In paragraph 10 two conflicting causes are identified for the 'threats to our common life': the first is that the American and Canadian churches 'challenged the standard of teaching on human sexuality articulated in the 1998 Lambeth Resolution 1.10' (which, until the Windsor Report, no one was aware was supposed to be obligatory); the second is the 'interventions in the life of those Provinces which arose as reactions to the urgent pastoral needs that certain [external] primates perceived'. 'The Windsor Report', we are told, 'did not see a 'moral equivalence' between these events...' Translated into the school-boy language which such trivialities merit, the interveners could plead, 'I wouldn't have hit you if you hadn't started calling me names'.

'What has been quite clear throughout this period is that the 1998 Lambeth Resolution 1.10 is the standard of teaching which is presupposed in the Windsor Report...' What this literally states is true; what it implies is a calm and deliberate lie. Those who acted in contravention of the Lambeth Resolution did so because they utterly disagreed with it in the first place, and had no reason even to suspect they were not fully entitled to do so. At one point in his address to the English General Synod on 26th February, Dr Williams suggests, 'This is a war no one chose'. He couldn't be more wrong: Dr Carey quite deliberately chose it. He could see popular opinion deserting the position it had held on the question of homosexuality for all his life-time, and opinion in the Church of England beginning to shift in the same direction. The Lambeth Resolution was a purely political stratagem, designed to prevent the English church from going any further down that road. The Primates in their recent statement deplore the innovations made in north America; but what has proved to be the biggest and most disastrous innovation of all is the suggestion Dr Carey clearly made, in particular to African bishops, that they had some kind of right to demand that the whole church was obliged to agree with their view on this question.

You would have thought by now that Christians generally would have woken up to the fact that the endless splits and divisions in Christianity are caused by the insistence, whenever disputes arise within the church (as they are bound to do from time to time) on the side that believes it has victory within its grasp being determined to impose its view on the whole body. Actual experience makes it clear that, in situations where apparently irreconcilable differences occur, a split can be averted by acknowledging – and tolerating – the disagreement; rather than rely on Lambeth Resolutions, or Windsor Reports, or Dromantine Declarations, if it is left to tolerant and free discussion, in time the disagreement resolves itself. Let me give an example. When I was a boy there was a fierce debate among the clergy as to whether capital punishment was a good or a bad thing, a necessity or a barbarity; those who argued the former, of course, had scripture on their side. Now, fifty years later, the problem has long been resolved – in favour of the unscriptural position – and no one feels the least concern about it. If Dr William is as anxious as he says to avoid a split, that is the advice he should be giving.

Instead, of course, he has systematically and unswervingly given ground to the African triumphalists, and fondly hopes that tears and beseechings directed at the other side will be sufficient to avert the catastrophe. At no point has he ever defended the *right* of those who disagree with the Lambeth Resolution to do so; the *right* of the north American churches to rectify what they see as the injustice – a very traditional and universally practiced injustice, but an injustice all the same – inflicted by the Church on homosexuals: not just the injustice of branding them as sinners, even when fully aware that Paul's understanding of the condition is faulty and that the condition itself is simply a part of nature and causes no problems to anyone; but also the injustice of attempting to impose celibacy on them as a condition of their acceptance within the community. We have all seen in recent years the consequences of imposed celibacy, some would say the inevitable consequence of such an imposition. The condemned innovations of the north American churches are a just and right

step towards rectifying these quite simply unChristian traditional views and practices – just as the condemnation of slavery
as unChristian was just and right, even though the New
Testament clearly stated otherwise.

'When gentlemen's agreements fail', Dr Williams asks, 'what
should we to do about it?' He will not like to be reminded of the
obvious English answer: 'Dissociate yourself from people who
clearly are not gentlemen'. His despair at the present situation is
not hard to understand. At one point in his speech he suggests,
'It is folly to think that a decision to "go our separate ways" in
the Communion would leave us with a neat and morally satis-
fying break between two groups of provinces... Every province
could break in several different directions.' There will be plenty
ready to reply, 'So be it. Such is the deserved consequence of
your own dithering and folly.' But in fact the prognosis is unduly
pessimistic – except in one particular area of the Communion:
the English provinces. In north America, and in English speaking
provinces generally, the liberals will be in a majority; in the now
notorious Global South, on the other hand, the conservatives will
prevail. In England it is not likely that either party can, or ever
will be able to, prevail. It has always been like this, which is
exactly why the Church of England has learnt the tolerance of
diversity that it has. What a pity, then, that it has failed to export
it, or that Dr Williams has failed to defend it. When the break
occurs (as now looks to be more or less inevitable) most Primates
will remain comfortably seated on their various thrones; it is
only the Archbishops of Canterbury and York who will find
themselves lying on the top of a mast.

If the Dar es Salaam statement is to be believed, it is the
Windsor Report that is to be the Shibboleth, as it were, that
separates the Ephraimites from the rest of Israel. Up to now the
American stance has been deliberately ambiguous – for
honorable reasons, let it be said. ECUSA as a body does not like
the report one bit, but also wishes to avoid a break if it can. It is

clear that such equivocation will not satisfy the primates. Which path therefore should ECUSA follow? It has always maintained that the question of the ordination and consecration of homosexuals, just like that of women, was essentially a question of justice rather than theology. Are the bishops now prepared to sully their consciences by taking the alternative view? If unity can only be maintained (and let us be clear, it is the conservative faction that have insisted on this dichotomy) by sacrificing the just aspirations of homosexuals, not just to be members of the church, but officiating members, and at all levels, then which option would a just and honourable body of men choose? 'Open your mouth for the dumb, for the rights of all who are left desolate.' Don't just nervously offer a minimal assent to this iniquitous Windsor Report; reject it, officially, wholeheartedly, unambiguously. If those trying to pressurize you into an unworthy submission break fellowship with you, is that really such a disaster? You will have delivered not just yourselves, but all of us, from a yoke of godly discipline such as we in England experienced during the Republic and never wish to see revived.

The Incarnation

Paul, a servant of Jesus Christ, called to be an apostle, set apart for the gospel of God which he promised beforehand through his prophets in the holy scriptures, the gospel concerning his Son, who was descended from David according to the flesh and designated Son of God in power according to the Spirit of holiness by his resurrection from the dead, Jesus Christ our Lord...
(Romans i.1-4)

It would be hard to find another passage of the same length in the New Testament which raises such huge question marks against the orthodox view of Jesus' nature and origin. There are two statements made on this topic, both of them apparently at variance with the traditional view. The first (*who was descended from David according to the flesh*) I don't propose to dwell on; the several inconsistencies on this topic that are found in the New Testament are all well-known and frequently discussed. There is first the point, which is clear from both the genealogies we are given describing Jesus' descent from David (in Matthew i.1-16 and in Luke iii.23-37) that the claim that Jesus was descended from David is inconsistent with the claim he was born of a virgin; and it is clear that both Matthew (i.16) and Luke (iii.23) are already aware of this inconsistency. Most modern readers would prefer to see Jesus as descended from David rather than as born of a virgin – for two reasons: descent from David implies nothing miraculous or particularly implausible, while not only is that not true of the Virgin Birth, but there is the obvious, and much more damaging, point that even if he had been born of a virgin, how was anybody going to know. But, sadly, even the claim that Jesus was descended from David, though (as the text of Romans above shows) it is undoubtedly early, cannot be accepted without question: there is a notorious passage in the synoptic gospels (Mark xii.35-37, Matthew xxii.41-46, Luke xx.41-44) which shows Jesus clearly rejecting such a claim for himself. The fact that the passage contradicts what we know was an early claim is the strongest possible argument that it is genuine.

What interests me much more is the second of the two claims: *designated Son of God in power according to the Spirit of holiness by his resurrection from the dead...* It would be tempting to see this as no more than the pious utterance of one determined to exalt his subject, and thus carried away in an exuberant burst of acclamation. But supposing it represents Paul's considered view of how Jesus became a divine being? Note, for instance, the contrast between the two claims: the claim to Davidic descent relates to Jesus as a human being (*descended from David according to the flesh*); and this is contrasted with Jesus' present status as a divine being (*designated Son of God...by his resurrection from the dead*). It looks as though both statements are intended to be understood quite literally; and if they are, the second of them has huge consequences for traditional orthodoxy.

What makes it seem likely that here we have possibly the earliest explanation of how Jesus became a divine being is that we find the same idea repeated twice in the Acts of the Apostles; and while that is not a particularly early work, it seems to preserve some of the ideas current among the earliest Christians, and which we find in no other New Testament document. The most obvious of these is the fact that the earliest Christians knew nothing of Jesus' life earlier than his baptism by John:

So one of the men who have accompanied us during all the time that the Lord Jesus went in and out among us, beginning from the baptism of John until the day when he was taken up from us...

(Acts i.21-22a)

You know the word which he sent to Israel, preaching good news of peace by Jesus Christ (he is Lord of all), the word which was proclaimed throughout all Judæa, beginning from Galilee after the baptism which John preached...

(Acts x.36-37)

Of this man's [*David's*] posterity God has brought to Israel a Savior, Jesus, as he promised. Before his coming John had preached a baptism of repentance to all the people of Israel.

(Acts xiii.23-24)

And Paul said, 'John baptized with the baptism of repentance, telling the people to believe in one who was to come after him, that is, Jesus.'

(Acts xix.14)

This realization explains why Mark, our earliest gospel, begins his account at that point. It would also explain why our two accounts of the birth of Jesus cannot be reconciled with each other. Both accounts are agreed that Jesus was born in Bethlehem – an absolutely necessary feature of the story in view of Old Testament prophecy (Micah v.2 – *see* Matthew ii.6); but there is no agreement between them as to how Jesus' parents got there. In Matthew the family is resident in Bethlehem anyway – he needs no invention of any kind of census to get them there; they leave only when they are warned about the threat to their child's life two years later, and are reluctant to return when Herod dies for fear that his son and successor may be just as bad; that is how they end up in Nazareth. In Luke, on the other hand, the family is resident in Nazareth; it is only because of the requirements of a census that they journey to Bethlehem, and once that is over they return to their native town. There is no need to reconcile the two accounts: the evidence makes it clear that both are entirely invented.

So let us compare what we find Paul saying here about Jesus' exaltation from an earthly existence to a heavenly one with what we find in Acts:

> This Jesus God raised up, and of that we are all witnesses. Being therefore exalted at the right hand of God, and having received from the Father the promise of the Holy Spirit, he has poured out this which you see and hear. For David did not ascend into the heavens; but he himself says, 'The Lord said to my Lord, Sit at my right hand, till I make thy enemies a stool for thy feet.' Let all the house of Israel therefore know assuredly that God has made him both Lord and Christ, this Jesus whom you crucified.
> (Acts ii.32-36)

The implication is unmistakable that for Peter Jesus has become Lord and Christ only after his death, and by virtue of his resurrection. And we find Paul implying the same later in the same book:

> And we bring you the good news that what God promised to the fathers, this he has fulfilled to us their children by raising Jesus; as also it is written in the second psalm: 'Thou art my Son, today I have begotten thee.'
> (Acts xiii.32-33)

Here God's declaration that Jesus is his Son belongs, not to his baptism by John, but to his resurrection.

Mark never makes explicit his view of how Jesus became divine, or indeed in what sense he was divine. We know that Matthew was dissatisfied with Mark's view by comparing these two passages:

> And as he was setting out on his journey, a man ran up and knelt before him, and asked him, 'Good Teacher, what must I

do to inherit eternal life? And Jesus said to him, 'Why do you call me good? No one is good but God alone.'
(Mark x.17-18)

Matthew finds the implication offensive; so he alters Jesus' reply to: *'Why do you ask me about what is good? One there is who is good'* (Matthew xix.17). Assuming that it is the beginning of both gospels which gives us the clue as to how the authors understood Jesus' divine status, it seems likely that for Mark it was the descent of the Holy Spirit on Jesus at his baptism by John that transformed him into a divine being. This suggestion that it is the Holy Spirit that effects the change is also what we find in the heading to the epistle to the Romans and in Peter's sermon in chapter ii of Acts. One suspects (one cannot say more) that for Matthew it is the Virgin Birth that has made Jesus a divine being – once again through the operation of the Holy Spirit:

When his mother Mary had been betrothed to Joseph, before they came together she was found to be with child of the Holy Spirit...
(Matthew i.18b)

The difference between the two views is fundamental. For Mark Jesus was a normal human being until seized by the Holy Spirit at his baptism and transformed into a divine being; that is the view that would later be condemned as the Adoptionist heresy, but there is little doubt that Mark substantially held it. For Matthew Jesus was born divine because of his paternity (for want of a better word) by the Holy Spirit.

So far we have encountered no mention anywhere of what Christians have come to call the incarnation, a notion that derives solely from the fourth gospel. For this author Jesus was not just born divine – like Mark, but for a different reason, he takes no interest in the birth stories at all; in this gospel Jesus is portrayed as having existed as a fully divine being from all eternity. His appearance on earth was a manifestation in time of a being that was part of God, as eternal and unchanging as God himself. This idea has been for centuries – for most Christians still is – a basic requirement of orthodoxy, so much so that for any professing Christian even to hint that he is unsure of its truth is to be marked out immediately as an unbeliever.

The basis of the insistence has always been that it is scriptural, which it undoubtedly is. The trouble is it is only one of four views (at least), all of which can authentically claim to be scriptural. Why should we insist on this one? But then, of course, why should we insist on any of them? One other thing they have in common, besides the fact they are scriptural, is that none of them can claim to be based on any kind of knowledge. Treated as imagery, which is what they clearly are, any one of the four is acceptable, and we need feel no compulsion to opt wholeheartedly for any particular one of them. It is the attempt to claim factual status for the imagery of the fourth gospel alone that is a major obstacle to presenting Jesus in a light that people at large are going to find helpful. I was brought up by Irish nuns who were forever dinning into my ears: 'Tell the truth and shame the devil.' It is time we Christians began to follow our own advice.

The Resurrection and the
World to Come

The resurrection: what really happened?

Although we have four gospels in the New Testament, we have five accounts of the resurrection, the fifth of them put in writing earlier than any of the gospels; and here it is:

> For I delivered to you as of first importance what I also received, that Christ died for our sins in accordance with the scriptures, that he was buried, that he was raised on the third day in accordance with the scriptures, and that he appeared to Cephas [*Peter*], then to the twelve. Then he appeared to more than five hundred brethren at one time, most of whom are still alive though some have fallen asleep. Then he appeared to James, then to all the apostles. Last of all, also to me.
> (I Corinthians xv.3-8)

It is very noticeable that this account bears no relation to that of any of the gospels. First, there is no mention of the women or the empty tomb; but even more strikingly, Paul seems to take it absolutely for granted that all the appearances were visionary. He makes no distinction between the way Jesus appeared to him, which can only have been a vision, and the way he originally appeared to Peter and 'to the twelve'. (So has he never heard of Judas?)

I used to think, and it is obviously tempting to think, that this was the earliest and best tradition, and that the empty tomb and the 'solid' resurrection appearances owed more to later credulity than to original experience. But I don't any longer – perhaps it is just because the idea *is* so tempting that I am inclined nowadays to resist it. I'm much more persuaded that Paul, however much he claims to be relating what he also received, is in fact deliberately 'liberalizing' a story which, in the form he received it (just as it nowadays strikes any number of Bible-reading Christians), struck him as crude and unbelievable. One very persuasive factor in this argument is the insistence of three of the four gospels – the exception is Mark's – that the original disciples themselves balked at the idea of Jesus' having risen or being alive. And even in Mark's case, if we had the complete gospel (the authentic text ends at xvi.8, the rest being written by a later hand to supply what from earliest times was thought to be a missing conclusion), it is likely that he too would have attributed the same reaction to the disciples.

Personally I am not at all convinced we do not have Mark's conclusion. Matthew throughout his gospel, and particularly throughout the passion narrative, has closely followed Mark's account; so if we subtract the story in Matthew xxviii.11-15 of the guards going into the city to report what they had seen, and being instructed – and paid – by the chief priests to tell the world otherwise, I suspect that in verses 16 to the end we have the material with which Mark also concluded his gospel. What particularly persuades me of this is Matthew xxviii.17: *And when they saw him they worshiped him, but some doubted.* It is astonishing that Matthew could not see the obvious implication of that closing comment, 'but some doubted'; he could so easily have removed it without any reader being aware of it. After all, when he came to incorporate Mark ii.27 in his own xii.8, he cut out that very disturbing saying, *The sabbath was made for man, not man for the sabbath.* And again, he gives us Mark's recorded saying, *And whoever says a word against the Son of man will be forgiven; but whoever speaks against the Holy Spirit will not be forgiven, either in this age or in the age to come,* and he also includes the incident which relates to speaking against the Holy Spirit ('*It is only by Beelzebul, the prince of demons, that this man casts out demons*' –

Matthew xii.24); but he has totally suppressed – for obvious reasons – the example that Mark gives of 'a word against the Son of man' that will readily be forgiven:

> Then he went home; and the crowd came together again, so that they could not even eat. And when his friends heard it, they went out to seize him, for they said, 'He is beside himself.'
> (Mark iii.19b-20)

The kind of indiscretion we find in Matthew xxviii.17 is just the kind of thing that Mark unthinkingly included and Matthew would deliberately have suppressed. One can only wonder why in this case he didn't. Perhaps after twenty-eight laborious chapters he was telling himself, 'Thank goodness this is nearly finished,' and allowed his concentration to slip.

But the most damaging insinuation in connection with the gospel accounts of the resurrection is made by Luke:

> 'Remember how he told you, while he was still in Galilee, that the Son of man must be delivered into the hands of sinful men, and be crucified, and on the third day rise.' And they remembered his words, and returning from the tomb they told all this to the eleven and to all the rest. Now it was Mary Magdalene and Joanna and Mary the mother of James, and the other women with them, who told this to the apostles; but these words seemed to them an idle tale, and they did not believe them.
> (Luke xxiv.6-12)

Do we need to be reminded that, not just the ancient world, but almost the whole world up to modern times, has tended to have a low opinion both of the intellect and the capabilities of women? This was much worse in the ancient world than in the modern, it's probably truer to say it was worse in pagan culture than in Jewish, and worse also in Eastern than in Western Europe. We should note that Luke's gospel appears, not just from the prologue addressed to the almost-certainly-gentile Theophilus, but from many features of the gospel itself – particularly the extraordinary interest it shows in Samaritans, who were regarded with suspicion by Jews, and who also are never mentioned at all in Mark's gospel – to have been intended for a gentile (though newly converted to Christianity) audience. Even if Luke had never recorded the comment, it would immediately have suggested itself to any educated gentile reader, and it is this consideration which most probably explains Paul's anxiety to suppress any mention of the women who supposedly discovered the empty tomb.

So what are we to conclude about the original 'event'? On the one hand, I suspect that what the gospels tell us about how the belief arose is accurate; on the other, what they want us to believe about it cannot be true. The women were in a state of extreme anguish and extreme susceptibility; they saw the angel or angels who told them that Jesus had risen, but you and I, had we been there, would not have seen them. And the message that the women heard, if true in any sense at all, is certainly not factually true, and this in spite of the fact that the Christian proclamation has always insisted that it is. We shall examine other possible ways of dealing with this 'proclamation' in later passages.

Did Paul believe it to be factually true? I assume that he did, but the surprising thing is, as we shall see, that he rarely discusses it as a historical event, but usually wants to see it as a continuing event, firstly in the inner life of the believing Christian, to some extent also (but to a lesser extent) as part of the communal experience of the Christian congregation. Let me now substantiate these claims.

The Epistle to the Romans

For the moment I am interested in only one aspect of the epistle, namely what Paul has to say in it about the resurrection, which is principally this:

> For if we have been united with him in a death like his, we shall certainly be united with him in a resurrection like his. We know that our old self was crucified with him so that the sinful body might be destroyed, and we might no longer be enslaved to sin. For he who has died is freed from sin. But if we have died with Christ, we believe that we shall also live with him. For we know that Christ being raised from the dead will never die again: death no longer has dominion over him. The death he died he died to sin once for all, but the life he lives he lives to God. So you also must consider yourselves dead to sin and alive to God in Christ Jesus.
> (Romans vi.5-11)

Any reader trying to evaluate this will notice how it constantly slips between literal and non-literal concepts. The opening sentence, taken out of context, could be read, and by Christians often has been read, as a perfectly literal forecast of the death of each one of us, followed by our personal resurrection from the dead. (If we attach it to the preceding material – *We were buried therefore with him by baptism into death, so that as Christ was raised from the dead by the glory of the Father, we too might walk in newness of life* – it becomes clear that Paul is not talking about a literal death and resurrection at all, but of our baptism symbolizing a kind of death, and our new life thereafter as a kind of resurrection.) The traditional notion is surprising, perhaps not entirely believable, but perfectly understandable; but then the same cannot be said of the next sentence, since none of the original readers had actually undergone crucifixion. Though

113

Jesus' own crucifixion was a fact, the crucifixion of the believing Christian that Paul is here talking about can only be a metaphorical one; it looks like a vivid and exaggerated description of what it means to repent. The whole of this can therefore only be metaphor, though Paul may have hoped – as his disciples certainly hope to this day – that the idea will be sufficiently vivid in the mind of the hearer that its purely metaphorical status will scarcely be noticed.

The see-saw effect between the literal and the metaphorical is at its most turbulent, when Paul says, *...as Christ was raised from the dead by the glory of the Father.* We presume he intends to refer to a literal resurrection from the dead which he believes happened ten, fifteen, twenty years ago; but if the fact that *we too...walk in newness of life* is also a resurrection, this is not a literal resurrection. Paul *might* (we cannot be sure) be talking about a literal resurrection for each one of us when he says in the earlier excerpt, *But if we have died with Christ, we believe that we shall also live with him*; but when here he talks about walking *in newness of life* as a kind of resurrection, it cannot be the same kind of resurrection.

How 'dead to sin' are we in reality supposed to be? There's many an evangelical Christian who, when asked the question, will put a bright smile on his face and assure us that all his sins are utterly forgiven, and that he now walks in the risen life of the Lord. And it looks as though Paul would like to feel like that, but clearly he doesn't quite manage it:

> Likewise, my brethren, you have died to the law through the body of Christ, so that you may belong to another, to him who has been raised from the dead in order that we may bear fruit for God. While we were living in the flesh, our sinful passions, aroused by the law, were at work in our members to bear fruit for death. But now we are discharged from the law, dead to that which held us captive, so that we serve, not under the old

written code, but in the new life of the Spirit.
(Romans vii.4-6)

That's how things are supposed to be, but as the writing proceeds it becomes ever clearer that he feels himself to be by no means 'dead to sin':

What then shall we say? That the law is sin? By no means! Yet if it had not been for the law, I should not have known sin. I should not have known what it is to covet, if the law had not said, 'You shall not covet.' But sin, finding opportunity in the commandment, wrought in me all kinds of covetousness. Apart from the law sin lies dead. I was once alive apart from the law, but when the commandment came, sin revived and I died; the very commandment which promised life proved to be death to me.
(Romans vii.7-10)

What Paul says here about 'the law' (which basically means the religion of the Old Testament in which he had been brought up) many would insist is true of all religion, including Christianity. What is supposed to promise life in the experience of many actually chokes them to death; what is supposed to inspire virtue descends to the pitiless observance of rules which often seem to have no connection with virtue. Is it any wonder that Paul continues to feel so bad about himself?:

We know that the law is spiritual; but I am carnal, sold under sin. I do not understand my own actions. For I do not do what I want, but I do the very thing I hate. Now if I do what I do not want, I agree that the law is good. So then it is no longer I that do it, but sin which dwells within me. For I know that nothing good dwells within me, that is, in my flesh. I can will what is right, but I cannot do it. For I do not do the good I want, but the evil I do not want is what I do. Now if I do what I do not want, it is no longer I that do it, but sin which dwells in me. (Romans vii.14-20)

Hamlet tells us that he is *indifferent honest; but yet I could accuse me of such things as it were better my mother had not born me*; and I suspect most of us feel something like that about ourselves, and that is healthy. But the above doesn't strike most of us as being at all healthy. Hamlet certainly felt bad about himself as, to some extent, we all do; but not as bad as that. He gave himself credit for being 'indifferent honest': that means reasonably – though by no means perfectly – virtuous. But Paul doesn't seem able to give himself credit for any virtue at all.

So there is a double conflict in how Paul understands our response to Jesus' death and resurrection. Certainly he understood the death of Jesus in literal terms, as we still do today; probably, though not quite as certainly, he understood the resurrection similarly. Equally certainly we too will literally die; probably also, in Paul's thinking, we will literally rise again. But both our death and our resurrection are also understood in quite non-literal terms: we died to our former life of sin through our baptism, and our emerging from the water was (equally non-literally) our own resurrection to new life in Christ. But (and this bit tends to be obscured by the evangelical tradition in Christianity) both this death and this resurrection turn out in practice to be more of an aspiration than a reality: in practice we are by no means as dead to sin as we are supposed to be and we wish we were; and the same is probably true of our risen life in Christ.

I Corinthians

The relevant chapter is xv. We have already quoted from it at the beginning of the this essay; but its conclusion is what concerns us now:

Lo! I tell you a mystery. We shall not all sleep, but we shall all be changed in a moment, in the twinkling of an eye, at the last trumpet. For the trumpet will sound, and the dead will be raised imperishable, and we shall be changed. For this perishable nature must put on the imperishable, and this mortal nature must put on immortality. When the perishable puts on the imperishable, and the mortal puts on immortality, then shall come to pass the saying that is written:

'Death is swallowed up in victory.'
'O death, where is thy victory?
O death, where is thy sting?'
(1 Corinthians xv.51-57)

The passage is frequently read out at funerals, and is popularly thought to embody the Christian idea of the resurrection. If it is, that must be because it is not well understood. The key to the real meaning of the passage is the clause, 'We shall not all sleep.' The popular explanation is that when Jesus eventually returns to earth to set up his kingdom, there will still be some people alive to see it. But Paul means very much more than that: he means that he himself, and most of his readers, will still be alive at the time of Jesus' return. The fact that he died nearly two thousand years ago on the one hand, and that we are still awaiting the event on the other, means that we cannot claim to believe his message here literally.

Thus when he supposes that we who are still alive at the time 'will all be changed in a moment' from a mortal body to an immortal, he is simply guessing, and has been shown by the event to be guessing wrong. (And after all, how could he possibly have had any information on the subject that would have enabled him to guess right.) Paul gives us two Old Testament quotes in support of his prophecy, but one presumes he was quoting from memory without checking up (as was in fact quite common in his day and apparently incurred no disgrace), and neither of them is very satisfactory. The first 'quote' ('Death is swallowed up in victory') is not found in exactly that form anywhere in the Old Testament; modern commentators assume he is referring to Isaiah xxv.8: *He will swallow up death for ever...* The second quotation ('O death, where is thy victory? O death, where is thy sting?') is recognizably Hosea xiii.14, but when you turn to the original you find Hosea's meaning is precisely the opposite of Paul's. Here is the original:

> Shall I ransom them from the power of Sheol [the grave]?
> Shall I redeem them from death?
> O Death, where are your plagues?
> O Sheol, where is your destruction?
> Compassion is hid from my eyes.

The speaker is God, and he is expressing his extreme exasperation with the behavior of Israel; so far from proclaiming the abolition of 'Death' and 'Sheol', which is the implication in Paul's text, he is calling upon them to be the instruments of his punishment.

Ephesians, Colossians et cetera

What modern translations call the Epistle to the Ephesians is, in the early manuscripts of the New Testament, not addressed to any particular church; the opening greeting reads:

> Paul, an apostle of Christ Jesus by the will of God, to the saints who are also faithful in Christ Jesus: Grace to you and peace from God our Father and the Lord Jesus Christ.
>   (Ephesians i.1-20)

Scholars deduce from this, probably correctly, that it is not in fact a letter by Paul, but an exercise in 'imitation' (a highly prized art

in the ancient literary world), written by someone who knew the
Epistle to the Colossians particularly well. This would explain
the suddenly lavish and orotund style that the author of this
work, unlike Paul himself, typically displays:

> And you he made alive, when you were dead through the
> trespasses and sins in which you once walked, following the
> course of this world, following the prince of the power of the
> air, the spirit that is now at work in the sons of disobedience.
> Among these we all once lived in the passions of our flesh,
> following the desires of the body and mind, and so we were
> by nature children of wrath, like the rest of mankind. But
> God, who is rich in mercy, out of the great love with which he
> loved us, even when we were dead though our trespasses,
> made us alive together with Christ (by grace you have been
> saved), and raised us up with him, and made us sit with him
> in the heavenly places in Christ Jesus, that in the coming ages
> he might show the immeasurable riches of his grace in
> kindness toward us in Christ Jesus.
>
> (Ephesians ii.1-7)

There are two remarkable features in that third and last sentence.
The first is, we cannot be sure that the resurrection is being
spoken of in literal terms at all; it may be, but we cannot be sure.
What are we to make of the assertion that *God... made us alive*
together with Christ... and raised us up with him, and made us sit with
him in the heavenly places...? Are we to suppose this is any kind of
fact? In one of his letters Paul warns Timothy against a pair of
apparently unorthodox preachers:

> Among them are Hymenæus and Philetus, who have swerved
> from the truth by holding that the resurrection is past already.
>
> (II Timothy ii.17b-18a)

But that, surely, is precisely what is being implied by the passage from Ephesians. Nor is it unique:

> If then you have been raised with Christ, seek the things that are above, where Christ is, seated at the right hand of God. Set your minds on things that are above, not on things that are on earth. For you have died, and your life is hid with Christ in God.
> (Colossians iii.1-3)

Not a word is being said about our hope of a future resurrection. In both passages our own resurrection is explained *solely* in terms of something that has already happened in the past; and it follows from this that resurrection here is being understood solely as metaphor.

An additional puzzle is that both of these passages must be late; Ephesians because, if we are right about its being non-Pauline, it is unlikely to have appeared while Paul was still around. But even Colossians must have been written towards the end of Paul's life; chapter iv.7-18 make it clear that it was written from Paul's prison-house at Rome where, as seems to be implied by the conclusion of Acts (xxviii.30-31), he lived for his last two years. (We have no good reason to believe, by the way, that he was martyred, nor indeed that Peter was, nor indeed that the latter ever visited Rome.) And the text itself seems to indicate a late date:

> Of this you have heard before in the word of truth, the gospel which has come to you, as indeed in the whole world it is bearing fruit and growing...
> (Colossians i.5b-6a)

Had these documents been early, there would be no difficulty about their showing no interest in a future resurrection. It may surprise the reader to be told that the very earliest Christians had no need of a belief in their own resurrection, nor in any kind of life after death, the reason being that they seem to have expected in all seriousness that they would quite literally never die. The evidence for this view is admittedly meager, the only unambiguous statement being the following:

> Let a man examine himself, and so eat of the bread and drink of the cup. For anyone who eats and drinks without discerning the body eats and drinks judgment upon himself. That is why many of you are weak and ill, and some have died.
> (I Corinthians xi.28-30)

We needn't bother here with just what offense it is they are supposed to have committed. The significant point is that illness and death of members of the congregation is something that shouldn't be happening and requires explanation in terms of blame. And it is not difficult to see why. At one point Jesus tells his disciples:

> 'For whoever is ashamed of me and of my words in this adulterous and sinful generation, of him will the Son of man also be ashamed when he comes in the glory of his Father with the holy angels.' And he said to them, 'Truly, I say to you, there are some standing here who will not taste death before they see the kingdom of God come with power.'
> (Mark viii.38-ix.1)

It is worth noting also – besides the parallel of the above in Matthew xvi.28 – the following additional reference:

> 'When they persecute you in one town, flee to the next; for truly, I say to you, you will not have gone through all the towns of Israel before the Son of man comes.'
> (Matthew x.23)

121

And the references to Jesus' promised reappearance after his death to his disciples in Galilee, which we find in Mark (xiv.28 and xvi.7) and following him in Matthew (xxvi.28, xxviii.7, 10), if authentic (and they probably are), were more likely to have been foretellings of his return to earth than – as they are now interpreted – simply resurrection appearances.

There is no actual evidence for the following idea, but it seems a reasonable deduction from what evidence we do have: the earliest Christians took it for granted that they would live forever because any day now (see the whole of I Corinthians vii – and particularly verse 29 – for a graphic statement of this view) Jesus would be returning to earth as judge, and all baptized Christians would thereafter live forever in his kingdom. But then the problem would inevitably arise: so-and-so was to all appearances a *perfect* Christian, and now he is dead. Perhaps in the early days some unkind souls muttered that this proved he can't have been as good as he looked; but the problem would inevitably become so widespread and distressing that another solution had to be found, and thus arose the idea that those who had died as faithful Christians would be restored to life at Jesus' return. In the writings of Paul there is no idea anywhere of a life after death as modern Christians understand it; the dead are truly dead, and when Jesus returns will come to life again. The most important text for the traditional belief in life after death is the story of the rich man and Lazarus in Luke xvi.19-31; so far from being an authentic parable of Jesus, to the practiced eye this looks like an *anti*-Christian Jewish fable. The other main source of such a belief is the Apocalypse. The whole idea is otherwise untypical of New Testament thought.

Some readers may have noticed a certain conflict in the evidence put forward so far. The evidence cited for the idea that the earliest Christians believed that they would never die was I Corinthians xi.30; but the classic statement of the supposedly later belief that those who have died as faithful Christians will be restored to life and Jesus' return to earth is I Corinthians xv – apparently from the same document. However, if you read through what we now have as the two epistles to the Corinthians, it will be obvious to most readers that both are in fact collections of fragments, probably therefore from a series of letters that were many more than two; so, despite the fact that both passages now appear in one and the same document, we have no real reason to believe they belong to the same period of Paul's life.

There is, however, an unresolved – and probably unresolvable – question of chronology. In history it looks as though the early believers saw no need of a resurrection; it was only later the idea was hit upon. But in Paul's epistles the development seems to be in the other direction: it is the earlier epistle that place great stress on the idea of resurrection, which the latest ones make no reference to. The earliest epistles of all seem to be those addressed to the Thessalonians, and there we find the following passage:

> But we would not have you ignorant, brethren, concerning those who are asleep, that you may not grieve as other do who have no hope. For since we believe that Jesus died and rose again, even so through Jesus God will bring with him those who have fallen asleep. For this we declare to you by the word of the Lord, that we who are alive, who are left until the coming of the Lord, shall not precede those who have fallen asleep. For the Lord himself will descend from heaven with a cry of command, with the archangel's call, and with the sound of the trumpet of God. And the dead in Christ will rise first; then we who are alive, who are left, shall be caught up together with them in the clouds to meet the Lord in the air; and so we shall always be with the Lord.
>
> (I Thessalonians iv.13-17)

123

No less than I Corinthians xv, these seem to be the genuine words of Paul; but the differences between how he describes the resurrection there and here are very striking. Here there is quite an emphasis on the idea that those who are dead and have to be raised from the dead will have a kind of priority in time over those still alive; there is no similar suggestion in I Corinthians xv. Unlike there, there is no suggestion here that those still living will have their mortal bodies suddenly changed to immortal. Above all, in I Corinthians the idea has apparently been dropped that we are all going to be caught up into the air; perhaps a later and more reflective Paul found the idea just a little comic, as do some readers to this day. Unlike I Corinthians xv, there is little attention drawn to the passage in I Thessalonians in the Christian tradition, and many very regular worshippers are not even aware of its existence.

Before we leave this theme, we need to take yet another brief look at I Corinthians xv. The chapter looks to be a unity, interested in the resurrection solely from a factual point of view, historic fact in the first half (to verse 34), future 'fact' thereafter; but what then are we to make of the following extraordinary argument:

> Now if Christ is preached as raised from the dead, how can some of you say that there is no resurrection of the dead? But if there is no resurrection of the dead, then Christ has not been raised; if Christ has not been raised, then our preaching is in vain and your faith is in vain. We are even found to be misrepresenting God, because we testified of God that he raised Christ, whom he did not raise if it is true that the dead are not raised. For if the dead are not raised, then Christ has not been raised.
>
> (I Corinthians xv.12-16)

Firstly, it is gratifying to be reminded that there is nothing new in Anglican liberalism, and that even in the very earliest days of

Christianity there were sophisticates languidly observing that the resurrection could not be understood as any kind of fact. But more seriously, at first reading one wonders whether Paul hasn't got the argument the wrong way round. Shouldn't he be arguing, not that it is our resurrection that proves the reality of Jesus' resurrection, but that on the contrary it is Jesus' resurrection that proves the reality of ours? So strongly have many Christians – perhaps a majority – felt this that they have even insisted that that is what he is really saying. But, as we have seen, there are aspects of Paul's understanding of the resurrection which make this violent distortion of his argument unnecessary. What he must surely mean – I concede there is an element of conjecture in this explanation – is that we know we have risen from the dead (note the past tense) because of the way we feel, because of the joy we experience, because of hope that sustains us; we could not feel this way if Jesus had not risen from the dead. Such an explanation, though, exonerates Hymenæus and Philetus in a way Paul perhaps would not have liked; but the passage quoted above from Colossians, which gives good grounds to be regarded as authentic, goes a long way to exonerate them anyway.

More Important even than the Resurrection

The Christian tradition tends to emphasize the resurrection as the most important theme of the New Testament; to those very familiar with it, however, this is not the case. Even in the documents we have (which in many cases are not all that early) Jesus' expected return to earth seems to have far more importance than the resurrection itself. It may even be the case that the resurrection was originally not so much important for its own sake as it was the necessary preliminary if Jesus' promise to return was to be fulfilled. There is one text (but only one) where this idea is actually explicit:

The times of ignorance God overlooked, but now he commands all men everywhere to repent, because he has fixed a day on which he will judge the world in righteousness by a man whom he has appointed, and of this he has given assurance to all men by raising him from the dead.

(Acts xvii.3-31)

Acts is not a particularly early document, but it appears to witness accurately to some very early themes in the Christian tradition, most notably to the fact (consonant with Mark's gospel, but in contradiction to Matthew and Luke) that the earliest Christians knew nothing of Jesus' life earlier than his baptism by John (i.22, x.37, xiii.24-25 etc.) We can accept with some confidence, therefore, its account of the earliest Christian preaching, which we find in Acts ii.14-36. The passage is too long to quote in full, but the sequel is in any case what chiefly concerns us:

Now when they heard this they were cut to the heart, and said to Peter and the rest of the apostles, 'Brethren, what shall we do?' And Peter said to them, 'Repent, and be baptized every one of you in the name of Jesus Christ for the forgiveness of your sins; and you shall receive the gift of the Holy Spirit. For the promise is to you and to your children and to all that are afar off, every one whom the Lord God calls to him.' And he testified with many other words and exhorted them, saying, 'Save yourselves from this crooked generation.'

(Acts ii.37-40)

Jesus' own resurrection is heavily emphasized, but there is no suggestion of a promised resurrection for the hearers; they are invited to be baptized for a wholly different purpose. It is, as the text makes clear, a baptism of repentance, a washing away of sins, so that when Jesus returns to judge the earth and destroy all the wicked, those that have been baptized will escape the dreadful fate that threatens all the rest. And the hearers fully understand the implications of what they have been told, which is why they ask, in an evidently anxious tone of voice, 'Brethren, what shall we do?' It is not so obvious from the text, but other parts of the New Testament make it clear, that the reason why they are not promised a resurrection is that there is no need of one; having been incorporated into God's kingdom they will live forever. I have already pointed out the frantic tone – not too strong a word – of I Corinthians vii:

> I mean, brethren, the appointed time has grown very short; from now on, let those who have wives live as though they had none, and whose who mourn as though they were not mourning, and those who rejoice as though they were not rejoicing, and those who buy as though they had no goods, and those who deal with the world as though they had no dealings with it. For the form of this world is passing away.
> (I Corinthians vii.29-31)

There can be little doubt that almost, if not right up to, the end of his life Paul was certain he would still be alive at Jesus' return, hence would never die. Those who had died in Christ would need to be raised from the dead – but henceforth to live forever; those still alive at the time would never experience death anyway, so had no need of a resurrection.

The crucial document for such information as we have relating to Paul's death is not so much the conclusion of Acts as II Timothy. The genuineness of this document has also been questioned – there aren't all that many that haven't!; however, for myself I am inclined to accept it, while conceding that I Timothy is more likely to be an 'imitation' along the lines that we suggested for Ephesians. The relevant passage of II Timothy is:

> For I am already on the point of being sacrificed; the time of

my departure has come. I have fought the good fight, I have finished the race, I have kept the faith. Henceforth there is laid up for me the crown of righteousness, which the Lord, the righteous judge, will award to me on that Day, and not only to me but also to all who have loved his appearing.

(II Timothy iv.6-8)

And the other passage that we need to note follows shortly after it:

At my first defense no one took my part; all deserted me. May it not be charged against them! But the Lord stood by me and gave me strength to proclaim the word fully, that all the Gentiles might hear it. So I was rescued from the lion's mouth. The Lord will rescue me from every evil and save me for his heavenly kingdom. To him be the glory forever and ever. Amen.

(II Timothy iv.16-18)

The first excerpt seems to be unambiguous evidence that Paul is aware that he has not long to live; and the second that he is in the middle of some kind of legal process. The two taken together are probably the main reason why the tradition maintains that Paul was martyred, but I would have thought had he really been so that the documents recounting his death would have been significantly earlier than in fact they are. A close examination of the text reveals considerable ambiguities. He is 'on the point of being sacrificed'; obviously, says the tradition, he is telling us of his approaching martyrdom – but that is the only hint of it. But, says the tradition, combined with the fact that he is obviously undergoing some kind of legal trial, that is the only likely explanation – except that Paul makes it clear that, despite the failure of his friends to stand by him, the hearing went well and he escaped the censure of the court. He clearly expects to be acquitted altogether: *The Lord will rescue me from every evil and save me for his heavenly kingdom.* Were it not for the earlier of the two passages quoted, we should assume this is a reaffirmation of his expectation that he would still be alive at Jesus' return; and we can't be absolutely sure that he doesn't mean that. But above all, note that there is no specific mention of any resurrection here, neither of Jesus' in the past, nor his own that is to come; all the emphasis is on Jesus' appearing – expressed even more vividly in the opening of the chapter: *I charge you in the presence of God and Christ Jesus who is to judge the living and the dead, and by his appearing and his kingdom...*

Finally there are those that argue that Paul shows clear signs in some of his writings that he no longer believes Jesus' return to earth to be as imminent as he once did. This idea has an obvious attraction in that Jesus' return never did in fact take place, but as far as I can see, the whole idea depends on a misunderstanding of a single text:

> Now concerning the coming of our Lord Jesus Christ and our assembling to meet him, we beg you, brethren, not to be quickly shaken in mind or excited, either by spirit or by word, or by letter purporting to be from us, to the effect that the day of the Lord has come.
>
> (II Thessalonians ii.1-2)

Once again there is an ambiguity. In our own day it is almost routine that every ten years or so someone will announce the end of the world and gather on that basis a highly suggestible and excited congregation; and it is probably just that kind of phenomenon that Paul is warning the Thessalonians against. But the Greek is unambiguously *that the day of the Lord has come* (perfect tense – possibly to be translated as 'is [already] here'), therefore a kind of present, but certainly not any kind of future, and certainly not, as the AV for instance has it, *that the day of the*

Lord is at hand. On the one occasion when Paul does use that expression in Philippians iv.5b (literally *The Lord near* – no verb) he is warning his hearers that it *is* the case, not that it isn't. The Vulgate has *quasi instet dies Domini*, which more or less agrees with the AV, and is probably indeed the cause of the error. Unaccountably the New Vulgate (1979) perpetuates it; but elsewhere the Catholic tradition makes the correction: the New Jerusalem Bible has *that the Day of the Lord has already arrived.* We need not doubt that Paul at the time was still expecting Jesus' return to be 'any day now', particularly as the epistles to the Thessalonians both appear to be quite early writings.

The way forward?

Inevitably, as we approach the end of the first century, a sense of disillusionment sets in:

> First of all you must understand this, that scoffers will come in the last days with scoffing, following their own passions and saying, 'Where is the promise of his coming? For ever since the fathers [*the first generation of Christians*] fell asleep, all things have continued as they were from the beginning of creation.' They deliberately ignore this fact, that by the word of God heavens existed long ago, and an earth formed out of water and by means of water, through which the world that then existed was deluged with water and perished. But by the same word the heavens and earth that now exist have been stored up for fire, being kept until the day of judgment and destruction of ungodly men.
>
> But do not ignore this one fact, beloved, that with the Lord one day is as a thousand years, and a thousand years as one day. The Lord is not slow about his promise as some count slowness, but is forbearing toward you, not wishing that any should perish, but that all should reach repentance. But the

day of the Lord will come like a thief, and then the heavens will pass away with a loud noise, and the elements will be dissolved with fire, and the earth and the works that are upon it will be burned up.

Since all these things are thus to be dissolved, what sort of persons ought you to be in lives of holiness and godliness, waiting for and hastening the coming of the day of God, because of which the heavens will be kindled and dissolved, and the elements will melt with fire! But according to his promise we wait for new heavens and a new earth in which righteousness dwells.

(II Peter iii.3-13)

This is one of the very latest documents in the New Testament. We needn't insist, by the way, that it is actually written by Peter; the very emphasis of the later part of chapter iii that it is is one of the major reasons for discounting its authenticity – that, and the fact, obvious from the argument, that it comes from a later generation of Christians than the first. (If the fathers have fallen asleep, how is it that Peter still alive?) It is clear there is a widespread acknowledgment, which the author is trying to oppose, that Jesus' return to earth will not be soon, perhaps will not be ever; such people are 'scoffers' and 'following their own passions', so should not be listened to. But nowadays there are an awful lot of such scoffers around (and I happen to be one of them). One of the nastiest features of the entire Christian tradition is the assumption that if anyone does not agree with you, it is because he is not merely wrong but wicked. There is no moral virtue in insisting that everything in the Bible must be understood to be literally true, and that any questioning of this is sin. On the contrary, it will be clear from the whole of the preceding argument that very little of the Bible can be insisted on as literally true: there is an awful lot of guessing, and much of it, as in this expectation of Jesus' return to earth, clearly mistaken.

Once we set aside the insistence that the Bible must be 'believed', it can be made to work as well for us as it appears to have done for previous generations – while so long as we hang onto that insistence, it doesn't seem to. There are lots of virtuous people, many of whom would even like to be thought Christians, who simply *cannot* believe the resurrection is any kind of fact – neither Jesus' original resurrection, nor our own promised one. No good purpose is served by insisting that in that case they simply don't qualify. One is reminded of the row in the early church, when it was still dominated by Jews, over whether Gentile Christians had to become Jews first before they could be incorporated into the Christian community. To the Jews it was 'obvious' that the new community was a Jewish one, and all members of it must have accepted the whole of Judaism; but the way forward turned out to be the opposite of that. Those who were Jews were not asked to abandon Judaism, those who were not were not asked to become Jews; in the event that worked well.

Paul's literal resurrection is hard to believe in, but his metaphorical one is as believable (and in fact as readily experienced) as ever. It is very likely true that Paul himself would not have accepted there was any distinction to be made between the two, but any modern reader can clearly see it and will not be satisfied by being instructed to pretend it isn't there. A traditional believer will tend to insist that it is only the reality of the historical event which gives actuality and power to the experience. For them it may well be so, but for the world at large this is a matter of individual temperament. The traditional believer is perfectly entitled to insist that without a literal belief in the original event, *for him* the new life in Christ would have no meaning; but he cannot insist on that for everybody else. Just as he himself cannot be contradicted, he cannot contradict those who find in their own lives that they get on well with a metaphorical resurrection, but cannot get on with the literal belief at all, who find that for them it is a hindrance rather than a help.

A major fault of the Christian tradition has been to claim knowledge and certainty where there can be no such thing, and to try and fix – by means of creeds and catechisms – the content of belief and the meaning of the Bible for all time. As regards the Bible, read naturally it would not only be interpreted differently in every age, but within each generation there would be multitudes of differing interpretations; this cannot be prevented and there is no reason why it should be. It could be argued that without a fixed and definite interpretation of the Bible the task of evangelism becomes all but impossible; if that is so, there are worse failings than a failure to evangelize. I am reminded of: *Woe to you, scribes and Pharisees, hypocrites! for you traverse sea and land to make a single proselyte, and when he becomes a proselyte, you make him twice as much a child of hell as yourselves* (Matthew xxiii.15). You cannot excuse telling lies simply with the plea that they are very successful lies. As regards the content of belief, the main failing here is probably the insistence on belief in the first place. Christianity should return to being what it originally was, a commitment to a way of life (Acts ix.2, xvi.7, xviii.25-6, xix.9, xxii.4, xxiv.14, xxiv.22); the story of the pursuit of orthodoxy is, and always has been, a nasty tale.

The enormous emphasis on the resurrection in the tradition, and the much more muted belief in Jesus' return to earth, are as we have noted the reverse of their order of importance in the New Testament; and it is no doubt because the promised return never materialized that this is so. Should we abandon the expectation of Jesus' return altogether? No, no need. Despite its almost despairing tone, and despite its utterly unconvincing plea that *with the Lord one day is as a thousand years, and a thousand years as one day,* the above excerpt from II Peter does show us how our commitment to that promise can still be valid. Look at the opening of the third paragraph: *Since all these things are thus to be dissolved, what sort of persons ought you to be in lives of holiness and godliness, waiting for* and hastening *the coming of the day of God...* It is those two words *and hastening* that for me redeem the whole idea; it is by the way we live our lives that we ourselves bring this coming day of God nearer. As with the resurrection, we do not need a literal belief in Jesus' return to earth; our own commitment to hastening the establishment of his kingdom for many of us works perfectly well. And for many of us this restores the priorities of the New Testament itself; hastening the arrival of the kingdom has far more relevance to our way of thinking than any belief in resurrection or a life after death. We need not be discouraged by the jibe that, however much we strive to hasten the arrival of the kingdom, there is no real hope that it will ever actually arrive. The more we strive towards it, the nearer it approaches; and the less we feel like bothering, the further it recedes.

B O O K S

O is a symbol of the world, of oneness and unity. In different cultures it also means the "eye," symbolizing knowledge and insight. We aim to publish books that are accessible, constructive and that challenge accepted opinion, both that of academia and the "moral majority."

Our books are available in all good English language bookstores worldwide. If you don't see the book on the shelves ask the bookstore to order it for you, quoting the ISBN number and title. Alternatively you can order online (all major online retail sites carry our titles) or contact the distributor in the relevant country, listed on the copyright page.

See our website www.o-books.net for a full list of over 500 titles, growing by 100 a year.

And tune in to myspiritradio.com for our book review radio show, hosted by June-Elleni Laine, where you can listen to the authors discussing their books.

MySpiritRadio